A Bloke Called Jesus

Also by Pro Hart and Norman Habel:
Outback Christmas

Also by Pro Hart:
Pro Hart's Waltzing Matilda (with Graham Jenkin)
Pro Hart's Breaker Morant (with Dawn Ross)
Pro Hart's Legendary Tasmania (with Paul William White)

Also by Norman Habel:
Scholarly Works
Reconciliation. Searching for Australia's Soul
Rainbow of Mysteries
An Inconvenient Text
The Tree Whisperer
Rainbow Spirit Theology

Job (Cambridge Bible Commentary)
Literary Criticism of the Old Testament
Yahweh Versus Baal: A Conflict of Religious Cultures
Powers, Plumes and Piglets: Phenomena of Melanesian Religion (Editor)

A Bloke Called Jesus

Paintings by
PRO HART

Text by
NORMAN HABEL

ATF PRESS
Adelaide
2022

National Library of Australia Cataloguing-in-Publication entry

Creator:	Habel, Norman, author.
Title:	A Bloke Called Jesus / Norman Habel
Cover design:	Myf Cadwallader
Layout:	Extel Solutions, India
Font:	Minion Pro, size 11pts

ISBN:	978-1-922737-25-0 (paperback)
	978-1-922737-26-7 (hardback)
	978-1-922737-27-4 (epub)
	978-1-922737-28-1 (pdf)

SCAN ME

Published and edited by

ATF PRESS

THEOLOGY

Making a lasting impact

An imprint of the ATF Press Publishing Group
owned by ATF (Australia) Ltd.
PO Box 234
Brompton, SA 5007
Australia
ABN 90 116 359 963
www.atfpress.com

Contents

Preface

I wrote *A Bloke Called Jesus* some forty years ago, working with Pro Hart to create a colourful portrayal of Jesus as a 'dinkum Aussie' from the Outback. Making Jesus into a true Aussie, back then, reflects a custom in many countries where Jesus is depicted by artists reflecting their culture and making Biblical figures relevant in their world.

The imagery of the poetry and the artwork reflect the bush, the Australian Outback with which I was familiar as a boy on a country farm. This Bloke belongs to my past and the traditions of my past as a descendant of white European settlers.

My identity as an Australian, however, has changed since I wrote this book. I am now more conscious that I am a part of a multicultural society in which the First Nations Australians are at the core. I am part of the colonial history of Australia and need to decolonise my mind if I am to become a true Australian in the future. In *A Bloke called Jesus*, Jesus is portrayed as a rough colonial bloke from the bush.

Admittedly, in the narrative 'At the Soak of Samaria,' Jesus the Bushman asks an Aboriginal woman for a drink. She replies,

> *How dare you ask for water from us*
> *after stealing the soul of this land?*
> *Have you come like a crow*
> *to abuse a tired old lizard?*
> *Have you, Bushman?*

In response Jesus, in this poem, claims that he is life from the Dreaming, life that is meaningful for women in pain like this Aboriginal woman. Jesus, the Bushman, says

> *Now is the time to worship God in the spirit,*
> *not in the mount of your ancestors*
> *and not where the white folks say,*
> *but wherever God is with women in pain.*
> *For God this day offers life*
> *through my spirit, my pain.*
> *I am the life from the Dreaming.*
> *I am the rain.*

If, today, I would pursue this image, I might portray Jesus as one of the First Nations people of Australia, not as one of the colonists, no matter how 'outback' he may appear.

Since Jesus was one of the people of the land back in Palestine, he could, of course, be portrayed here as one of the First Nations people of Australia. This volume, however, captures the imagery of the time and context in which it was written and, as such, it is an enjoyable read without necessarily changing the title to *A Colonial Bloke Called Jesus*.

Enjoy as is!

A Bloke Called Jesus

Who is this bloke they call Jesus
With his red prickle beard and his dog?
A prophet God sent to the Outback
Or a flamin' country mug?

You can ask the people of Cana
And they'll shout his name with a cheer;
At their wedding his fame started spreading
After changing their water to beer.

You can ask the sinners who heard him,
His eyes made them squirm in their shoes;
Some returned to their Father rejoicing
And others just took to the booze.

You can ask that larrikin Laz'rus
With his wild colonial ways;
For he knows what it's like to be living
After being a corpse for three days.

You can ask the wind of the desert
That has blown since the world first began,
From the time the blacks call the Dreaming
And now blows through the word of this man.

You can ask his twelve brave companions,
His good mates who saw how he died,
How they pierced his flesh with a spear point
Until water poured red from his side.

You can ask that lady called Mary
Who conversed with an angel or two,
Had a chat with a bright risen Jesus
And claims her wild story is true.

Should you ask my considered opinion,
Since I am his best mate, John,
From the things I have seen in his lifetime
I would say he is God's only Son.

John 1:1–14; 21:24

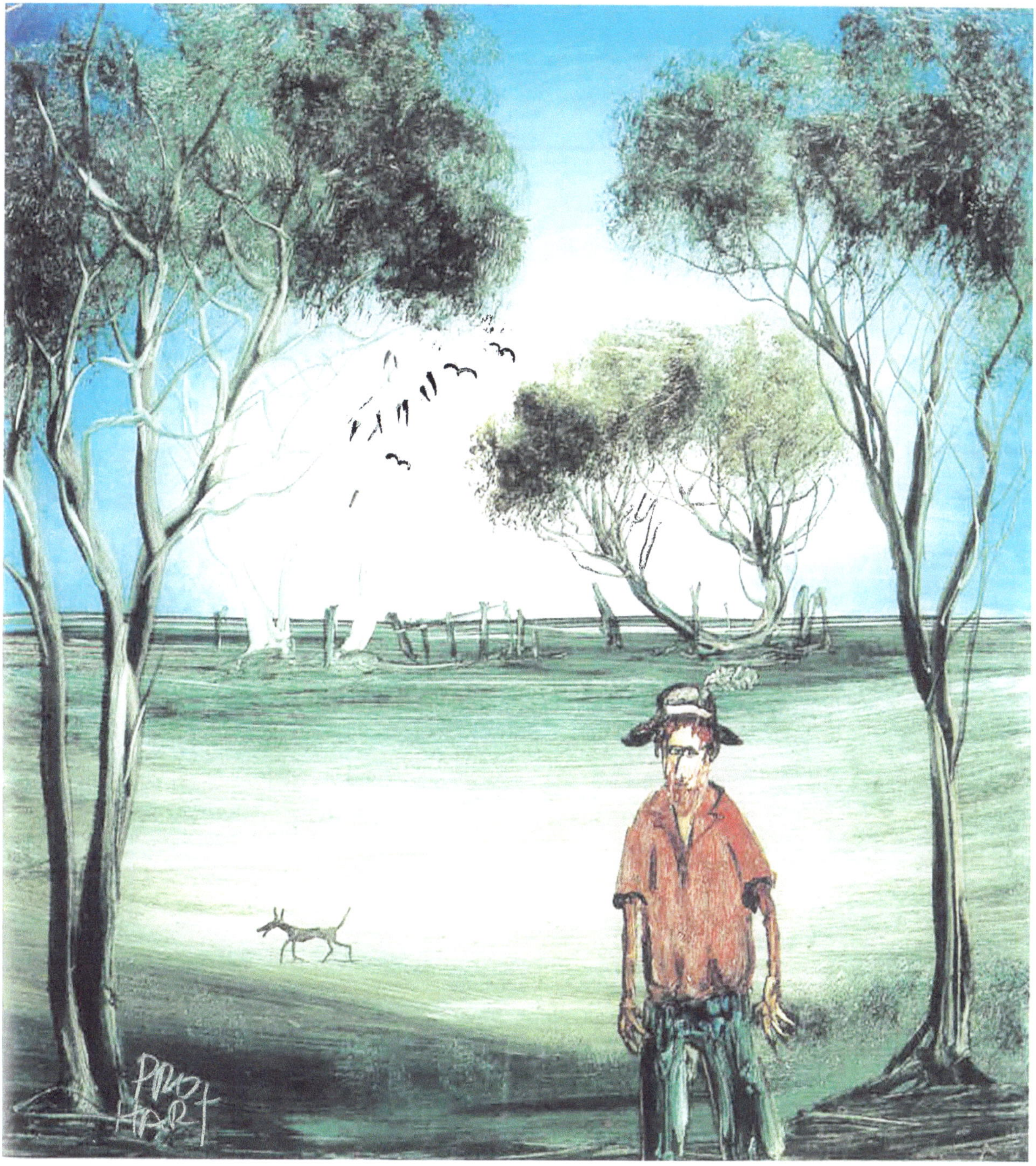
PRO HART

We Are His Mates

When Jesus rode in with his horse and his dog
And a couple of mates from out back,
We swotted the flies and sipped on our beers.
So why should we stir for this man or his God?

My name is Nathaniel, and mysbullock team
Knows the sound of my cursing in time with the whip.
So when Jesus yelled, 'Fellas, this bloke is true blue,'
The barman yelled, 'Mates, shout the new chum a beer.'

Now Simon the Rock was one of his mates,
And Andrew his brother, both whalers down South.
'This chap is the Bushman long promised,' said Rock.
'The man from the Dreaming who knows about God.'

'Where do you come from?' cried someone in jest.
'From Nazareth out back,' said Rock with a grin.
'The dingoes,' I said, 'Refuse to die there.
What good can come out of that dead country town?'

'Nathaniel, I know you,' said Jesus straight out.
'Where in hell,' I replied, 'have we met on the track?'
'In the Dreaming,' he said, "neath a black wattle tree,
I saw you, I chose you to learn about heaven.'

'Which trail leads to heaven,' an old drover quipped.
Said Jesus, 'Love God and your mates to the end.'
'And who is my mate? the old drover yelled back.
'I'll tell you a story,' said Jesus again.

'A bloke from the city came travelling out back
When bushwackers hit him and left him half dead.
Along came a trooper and called to the bloke,
"Which way did they go? I'm hot on their tracks."

'Then came a drover who yelled to his dog,
"We best keep away from this whole bleedin' mess."
But the black who came next brought the bloke to this pub.
Now who was a mate to the poor chap, my friends?'

We followed this Bushman, this Jesus from God,
And we learned what it meant to be loyal and free.
For we are with Jesus and we are his mates
And we'll stick with our mate to the end.

John 1:43–51
(cp. Luke 10:29–36)

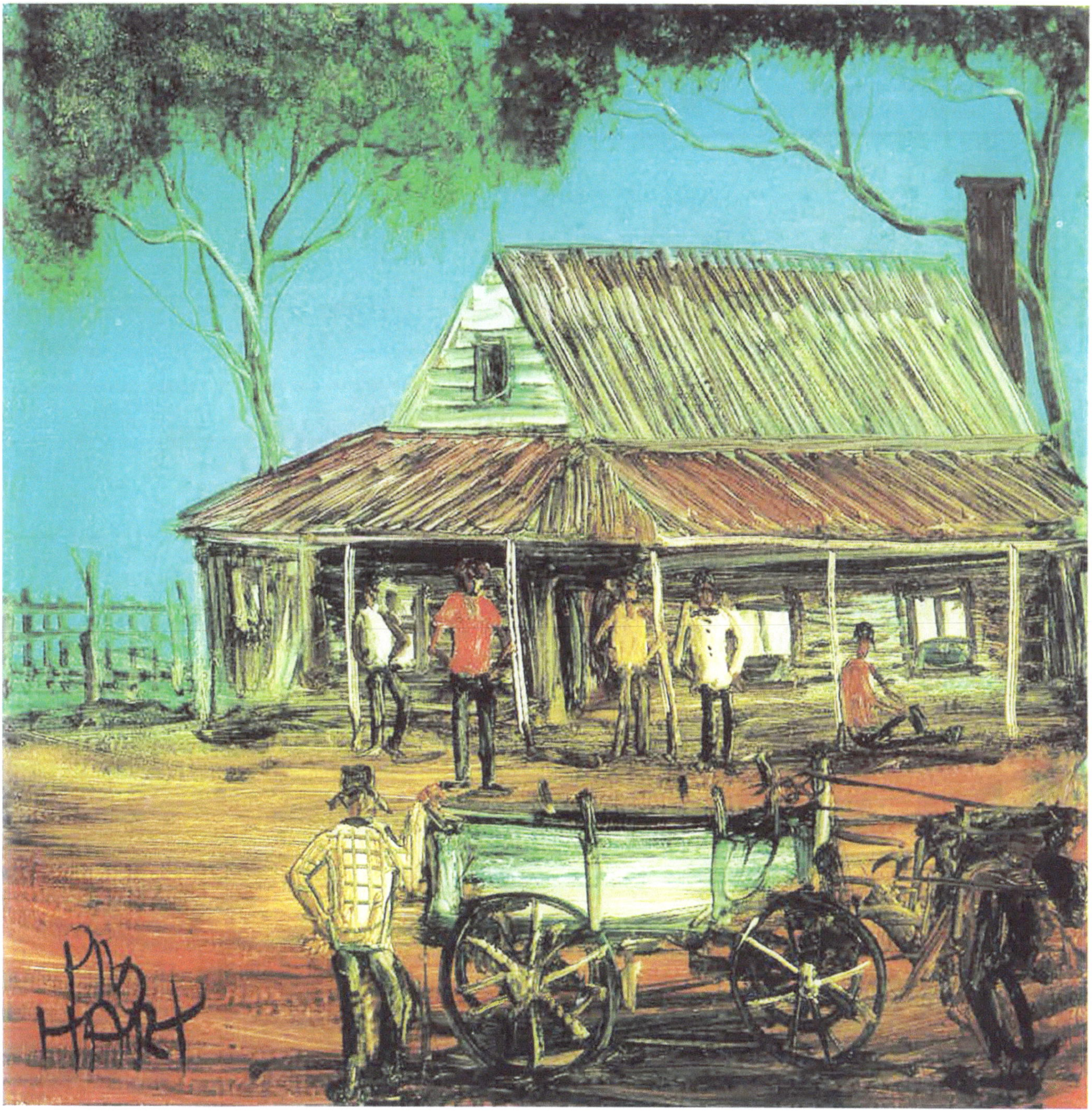

The Tin Kettling at Cana

Oh, the tin tin kettling at Cana,
Oh, the do at the old shearing shed,
When the story of Jesus caught fire
And the glory of the Bushman spread.

Oh, the loud bang, banging of tin cans
When the bride and groom first came,
With the sheep all bleating their welcome
And the dogs all howling with pain.

Oh, the screams and shrieks in the woolshed
When the boys let the cockatoos go,
As they swiped at the birds with straw brooms
Till their feathers were falling like snow.

Oh, the shame of the bride's poor parents,
When they toasted the groom with a cheer;
It was not that the jokes had been dirty,
But the shame of a shed without beer.

Oh, the wild wild yahoo when Jesus
Grabbed the best man out by the door
And told him to fill every barrel
With the water from a dirty old bore.

Oh, the shouts and cheers from the stockmen,
When the blokes with the kegs reappeared,
As jug after jug kept on flowing
With a glorious golden brown beer.

Oh, the songs and grand celebration
For the miracle Jesus had done;
Making beer out of dirty bore water
Was as great as God stopping the sun.

John 2:1–11

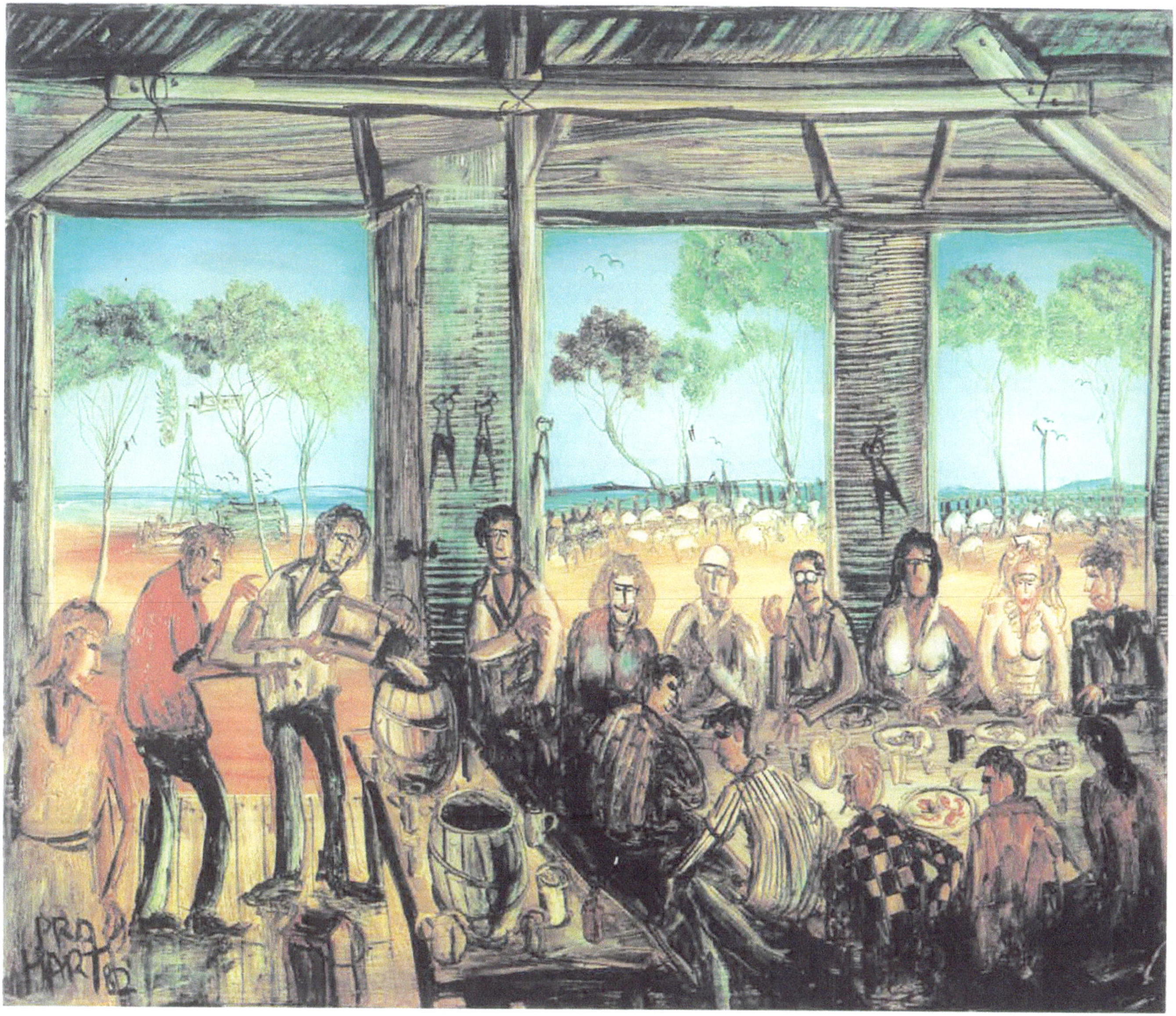
PRO
HART 82

At the Soak of Samaria

My skin was weathered
like a desert lizard at death;
my soul was dry deep down,
shrivelled by wind and whites
who poured our blood
on the ochre earth
where once the lizard people
sunned themselves with pride.

I wandered slow that day
across the fierce noon sands
to the soak my father had dug
with his mulga walking stick.
He was the first lizard-man
who walked this empty land
to fill it with trails of life.
That mountain out yonder
is the site where his old body fell.
His spirit lives on in the soak
but the flow of his life
is slow now, slow.

Near the soak the Bushman sat
with his empty water bag.

'Give me a drink,' he said.

'How dare you,' I snarled,
'ask water from us
after stealing the soul of this land?
Have you come like a crow
to abuse a tired old lizard?
Have you, Bushman?'

'If you knew who I am,' said the man,
'you would ask for my gift,
the water of life from above.'

You fool,' I replied,
'this soak is now buried in sand,
and whites cannot find
the water below.
So how could you give me water?
Are you greater than our father,
who came in the Dreaming
to dig this soak
for wallabies and women out back?'

'The water I give,' said the man,
'will well up within
like a spring in your deep dry soul.'

For a moment I hoped
that the man from the bush
might offer a flask of rum
to revive my battered brown body

'Woman! Woman!' he said,
'You have slept with whites.
You have slept with blacks.
You have emptied your soul
to find cheap grog.
Now you're only a skin,
a dry hollow skin.'

That was the instant I knew
the burning eyes of the Bushman
could read my mind, my fears,
my life.
I wanted to know his magic,
his promise of life.

Now is the time,' said the Bushman,
'to worship God in spirit,
not in the mount of your ancestor
and not where the white folks say,
but wherever God is
with women in pain.
For God this day offers life
through my spirit,
my pain.
I am the life
from the Dreaming.
I am the rain.'

The water from the soak
that day
. . . was sweet.

John 4:1–42

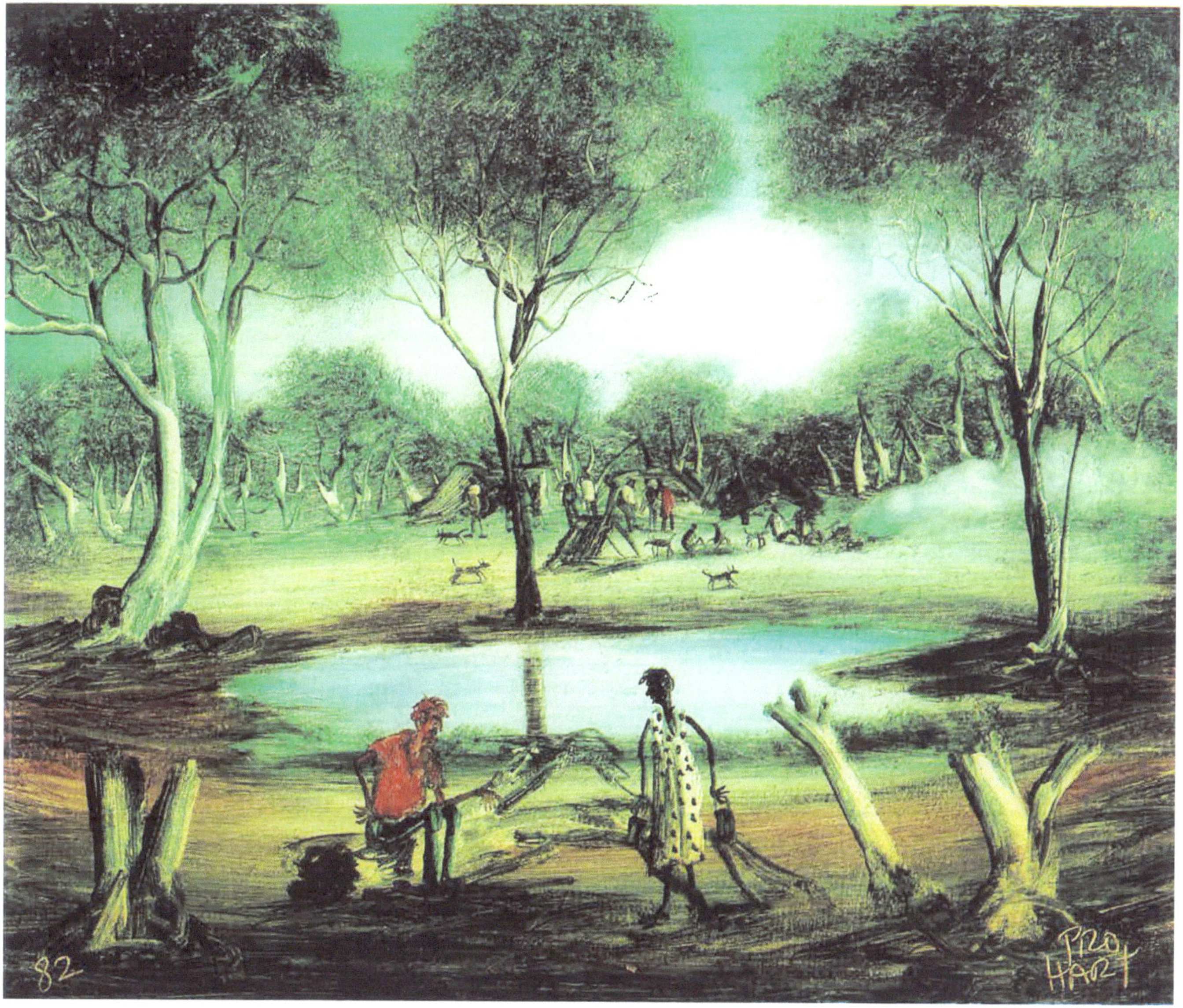
82
PRO
HART

Sign at the Shearing Shed

Back forty years, I was good,
Gun shearer, set to be king.
A ringer I was at twenty-one,
My blades as fast as wings.
The roustabouts all gaped,
The boss cockies stood in awe
As I poured each fleece like water,
White waves on the greasy floor.

Then disaster struck my bones,
My joints went tight as drums,
My body a bundle of pain,
A cripple at twenty-one.
Beside the skirting table
With half the classing done,
I'd long to be up front,
Where the race for ringer was on!

Old drovers swore the spring
That gurgled behind the shed,
Would heal the first bloke washing there,
When it bubbled and blew its head.
To reach it took too much pain,
To help took too much trouble;
The tales old drovers told were tall,
The spring but froth and bubble.

When Jesus the Bushman arrived
I shoved some shears in his hands,
'I'll take you on, big Jesus!
Twenty ewes or ten old rams?'
'You still want to shear,' asked Jesus,
'And cover the floor with fleece?'
'My oath, my bloody oath,' I laughed,
'But youth is beyond my reach.'

'Get up and walk,' said Jesus,
As if he were God let loose;
I looked him straight in the eye.
My God, he was telling the truth!
A gurgling rose inside my body,
A bubbling deep within
Till all my joints were free
Like a baby cleansed of sin.

'Well, starve the lizards,' I yelled,
'It's like I was twenty-one.
Come, grab your blades, you Bushman.
It's time those rams were shorn.'
'No way,' the shearers cried,
'No shearing after five!
That's the law of the shed round here—
The dog who breaks it dies!'

'You've just seen God at work,'
Said Jesus, set for a fight.
'The God who makes stars above,
He never knocks off at night.
Forget the tally and the run,
And let this new man be,
It's life that matters, not the law,
When I have set you free.'

John 5:1–18

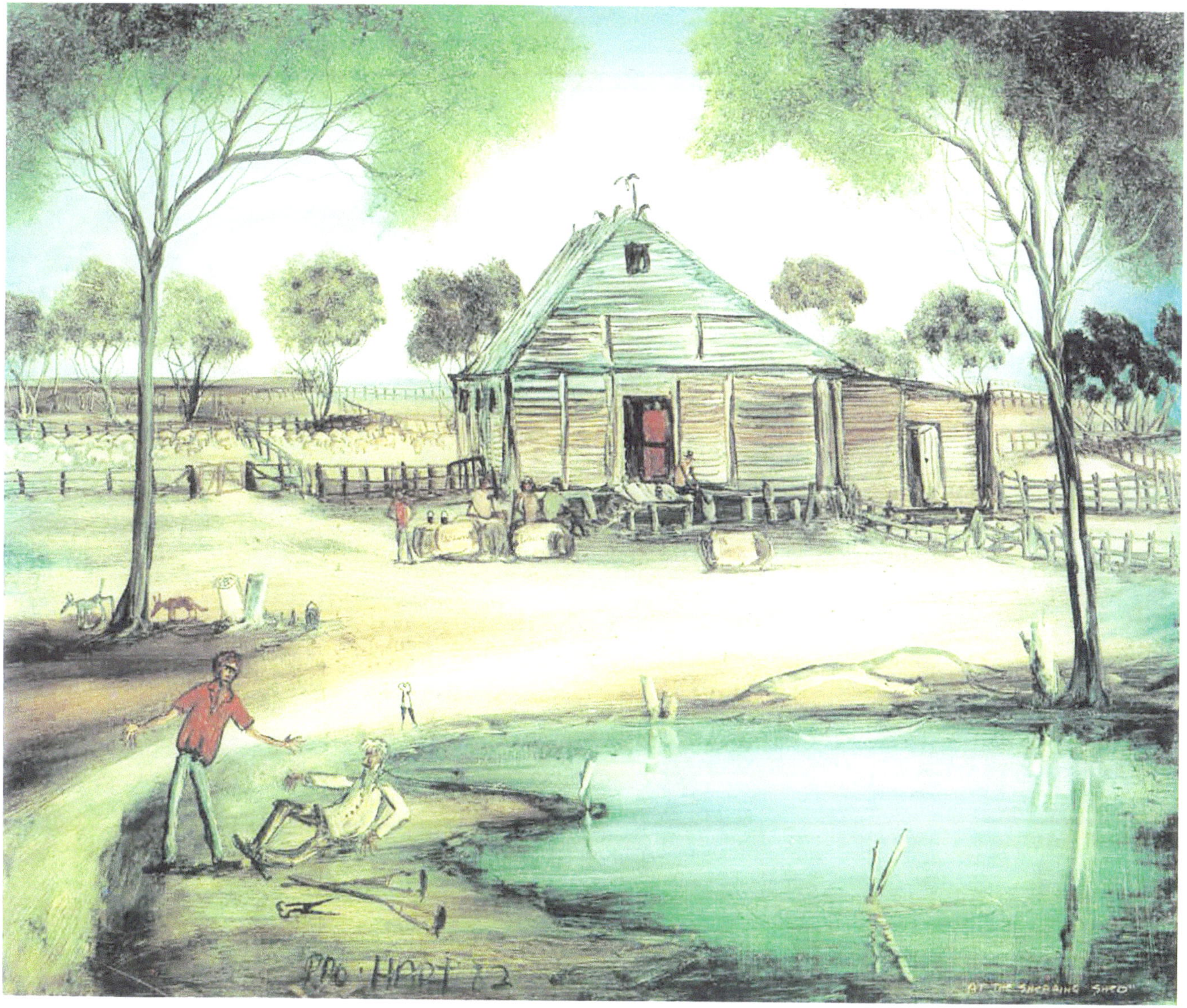
PRO HART 72
"AT THE SHEARING SHED"

Picnic at the Races

Life was hot and dry that year
and many folks were ill,
yet all the bush rode in
to celebrate the races
on the dry creek bed out back.

That's the year when Jesus came
and was urged to 'ave a go.
'Your nag looks like a cross
between a brumby and a mule,' they yelled.
'Bet he never makes it round the track.'

Jesus just winked at his horse,
Sat down in the shade,
and healed little kids of their pains.
He spun out his yarns about God
and his love for sinners out back.

Late in the dusk I heard someone yell,
'Heh, let's have a bite to eat.'
'You silly old coot,' another bloke said,
'The scones are all gone
and there's nothing out here
unless you've a liking for snake.'

So I came close to Jesus and timidly said,
'Mr Bushman, please sir,
me Mum made a damper for lunch
and I caught some yabbies down by the creek.
Would they do instead of fresh scones?'

The people all sniggered and I hid my face,
but Jesus said, 'Son, they will do.'
He broke up the damper and handed it round
till the bush folk had eaten enough;
even my yabbies, well-cooked by the sun,
were shared by the kids from the scrub.

'Don't work so hard for the food that decays,'
said Jesus, off preaching again.
'Work for the food that endures beyond death,
the food from the Bushman of God.'

'We battle the drought,' said a withered old man,
'and we work bloody hard to survive.
How dare you degrade the work of our lives.'

'I am the damper of God,' said the Bushman,
'sent here to give you life;
those who eat me, my flesh and my blood,
will rise from the dust
and return to the Dreaming with God.'

'You're a Bushman,' they cried,
'A country mug from Galilee,
and not from the Dreaming or God.
A miserable meal you'd make, anyway,
as tough as a wild camel steak.'

When Jesus went home from the races
we ran round the hill
with an old billy can,
and would you believe,
we collected twelve billy cans full,
full to the brim
with delicious sun-baked yabbies.

I mean,
would you believe it?

John 6:1–58

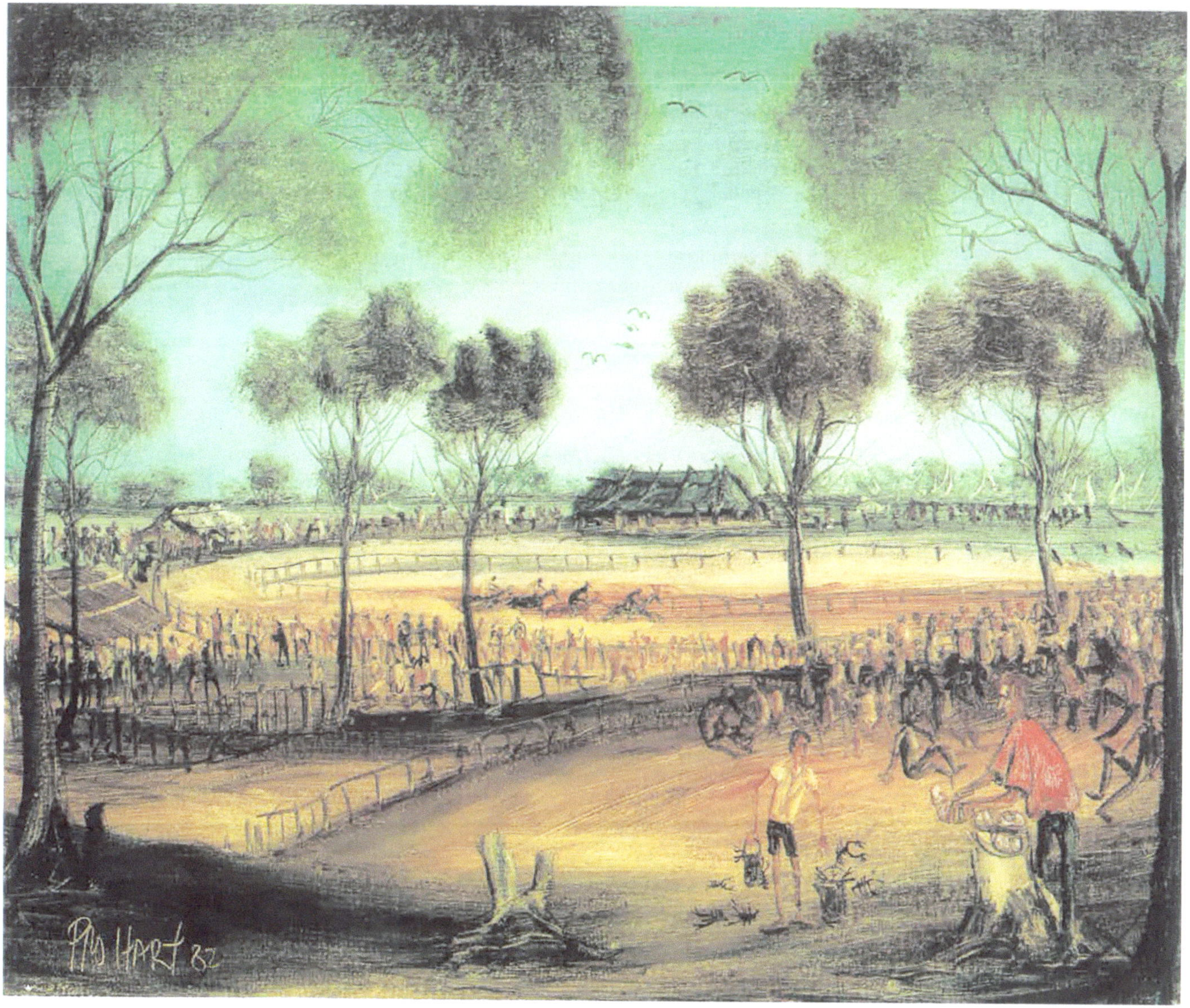
Pro Hart '82

A Song for Stoning

We would walk as children
through the white limestone rocks
that cluttered the gasping ground
and pelt them with glee at rabbits,
mice, or an old black stump
with a face like the devil
conniving,
eyeing,
conniving with us in our sins
and rousing our song of guilt:

> White stones, white stones,
> to break your bones
> and chase the devil away.

When a sleek brown snake
would weave its way towards us,
eyeing,
sliding,
eyeing us from rock to rock,
we would throw fast stones
and pelt it with shouts of power:

> White stones, white stones,
> to break your bones
> and chase the devil away.

Years later, I, a bitter barmaid
among the hot seductive rocks
and goldfield towns out back,
could hear the tongues of pious wives
sliding,
twisting,
sliding back and forth their curse
on me, a devil they could hate:

> White stones, white stones,
> to break her bones
> and chase the devil away.

The night they stormed my room,
I slept with a squatter's lonely son.
'Leave town, you bitch,' they screamed.
then asked the Bushman for a verdict,
twisting,
yearning,
twisting words to justify a death
and let them revel in their song:

> White stones, white stones,
> to break her bones
> and chase the devil away.

Jesus drew a line across the dust.
'Let any free from sin,' he called,
'throw the first white stone.'
The angry crowd looked on
yearning,
squirming,
yearning for the sound of falling stone;
instead they heard the Bushman say,
'I set you free, now sin no more,
and remember what I say':

> Throw stones, white stones,
> if you alone
> have never sinned that way.

The angry guilt of those in town
reached fever pitch that night
when Jesus called them liars.

'I am before you all,' he said,
'I am before old Abraham.
I am from the Dreaming
and if you trust in me,
you too will live forever.'
'This dog is the devil himself,'
they whispered,
eyeing,
conniving,
eyeing him like a snake for stoning
and a chance to sing their hate:

> White stones, white stones,
> to break his bones
> and chase the devil away.

They took up stones to throw at Jesus
but he merged with the rocks
and was gone with the dusk
leaving his song
for all who take up stones to judge:

> Throw stones, white stones,
> if you alone
> have never sinned that way.

John 8:1–59

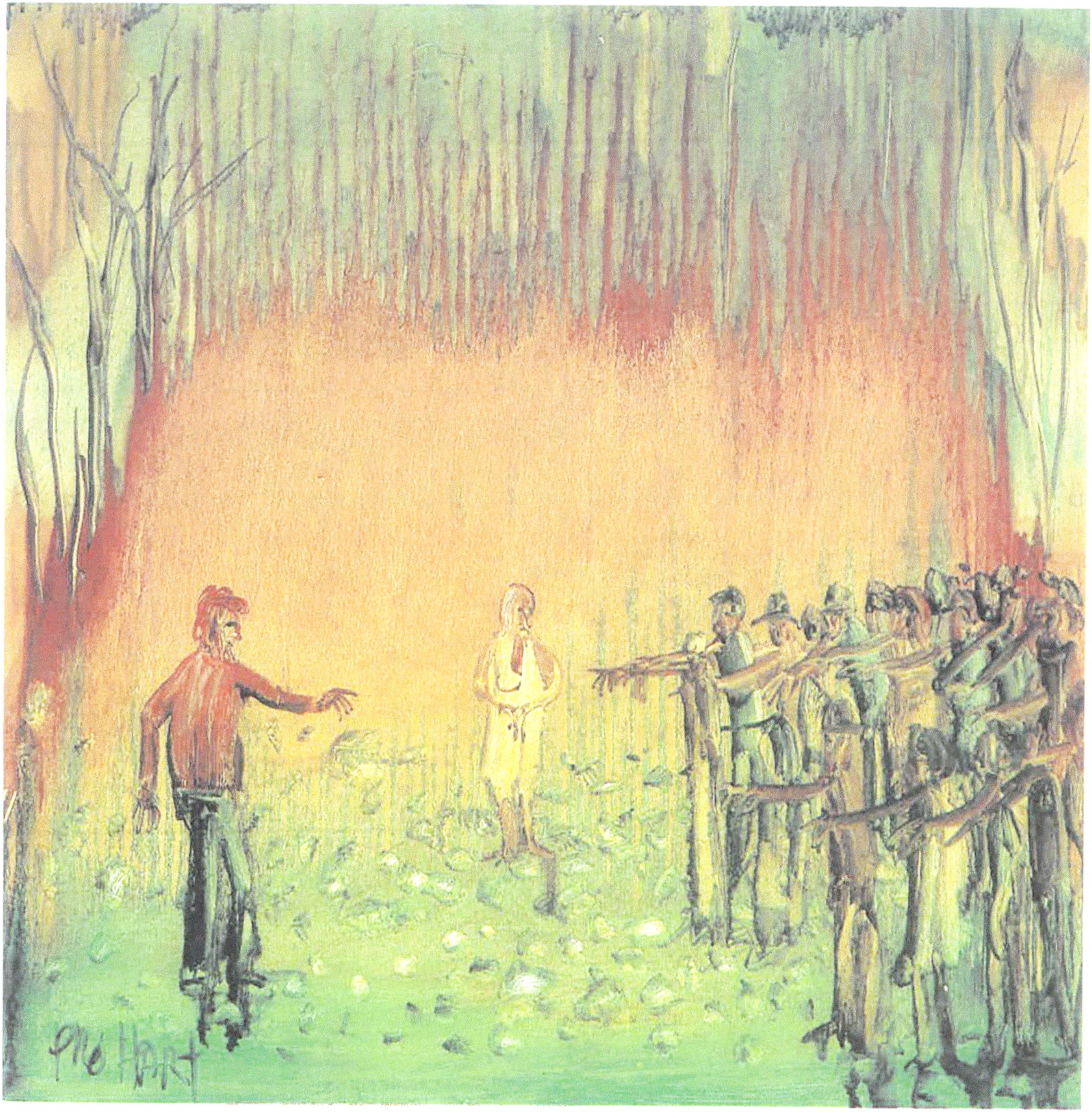
Pro Hart

I am the Good Drover

When the blind man was healed
The Outback was burning with gossip.
Who was this man?
A demon released from a cave?
A mad country drover
Hit by the heat of the sun?
Then Jesus began his new droving song
As he poured out a drink for his dog
In the top of his old bushman's hat:

Keep drovin', keep drovin'.
I am the good drover.
Through sandhills and salt pans,
I drove on forever.
When heaven is empty
And stars are cold silent,
I drove through the shadow of death.

I'll drove all your crying,
I am the good drover.
I'll drove all your doubting,
I drove on forever.
In fear of the darkness,
The snake-biting darkness,
I drove through the gorge of despair.

I'll drove when you break out,
I am the good drover.
I'll drove your rebelling,
I drove on forever.
My stockwhip keeps singing
It's song to the straggler,
I'll drove to the sheltering tree.

I camp by the good grass,
I am the good drover.
I travel on quickly
When back roads are barren.
I search through the distance,
The dry desert distance,
I drove where the water is life.

I lay down my life, friend,
I am the good drover.
I take up my life
To give over and over.
And if you but follow me
As the good drover
I'll suffer the drought lands with you.

At night round the campfire,
I am the good drover,
I'll tell you my dying
And laugh till it's over.
And if you but listen
Above the dark silence,
My laughter will rise in your soul.

I come from the Dreaming,
I am the good drover.
I'll send you my spirit
To lead you forever.
The wind will surprise you,
Like sheepdogs will guide you
And drove through the Dreaming with me.

John 10:1–10

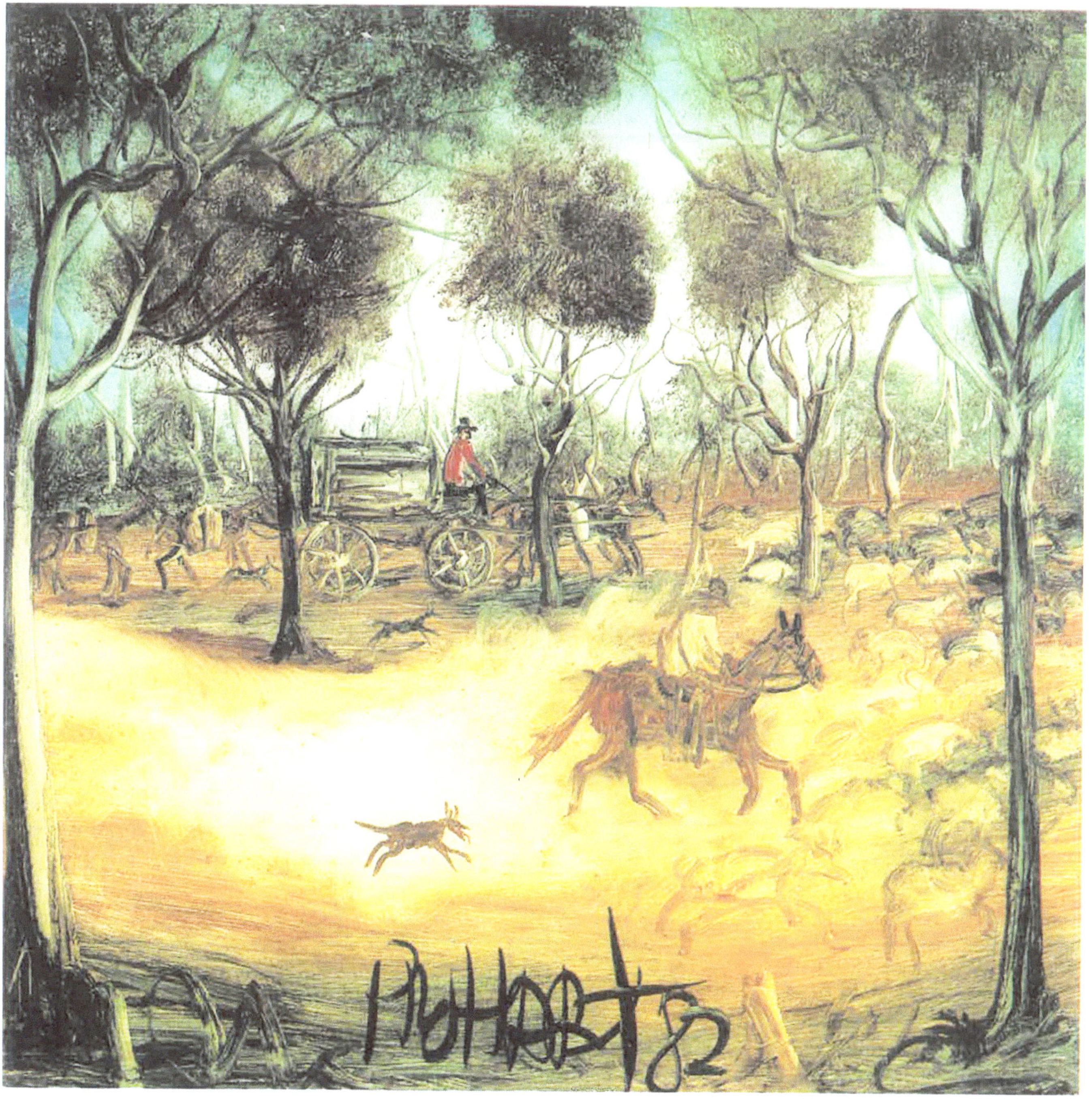

That Larrikin Lazarus

That Larrikin Laz,
My bothersome brother,
Was always embarrassing me—
Well, Mary and me.
He never did what he was told.
Yet everyone loved our Bethany Boy
With his wild colonial ways.

When our brother fell ill
From some sickness he found
On one of his triumphs in town,
We notified Jesus to come.
He came, but too late.
The Bethany Boy was dead.

I laid out the body myself.
I did it all proper, I did.
I washed every part.
I blocked it all up
And smeared it with fine liniment.

Beside him I laid his boots and his hat
And covered his face with a blanket.
It was lucky,
In view of what happened next day,
That Laz was laid out in his pants.

When Jesus arrived
I raced down the track.
'You should have been here,' I yelled,
'and Laz would never have died.'
'Your Lazarus will rise,' said Jesus.
'Can you believe that, Martha?'

'At the end of the world,' I replied,
'When it's too flamin' late, he will rise.
He ought to be living right now.'

Jesus said, 'Martha,
I am the rain,
The resurrection, the rain.
I'll splash on your dust.
You'll dance on your grave.'

'I know you're God's Son,
Bush King and all that,
But you should have been here,'
I replied.

'That rock,' said Jesus, 'remove it!
The rock at the face of the cave.'

'Now Jesus,' I said,
'He's been dead four days.
He'll stink like an old rotting cow,
In spite of my fine liniment.'

'Just watch me,' said Jesus,
'1'11 show you God's glory at work.'

He prayed for a while
And gave out a yell
That would waken the flaming dead.
It rang through the valley
Till all the bushland was still.

Out from the cave
Came a flutter of bats,
A couple of grumpy goannas,
A tumble of toads,
And a rather disgruntled night owl.

At the end of the line
Came Laz in his glory,
Holding his boots in one hand
And his greasy old hat in the other.
Two large plugs of wool
Stuck out from his ears—
At least he was wearing his pants.

How embarrassing it was,
This corpse coming out
With a dirty wry grin on its face
And a greeting for Jesus,
'Well, how are you mate?'
And a question for me
'Say, Martha my dear,
Is there tucker back home?
I've a hangover
You wouldn't believe.'

John 11:1–44

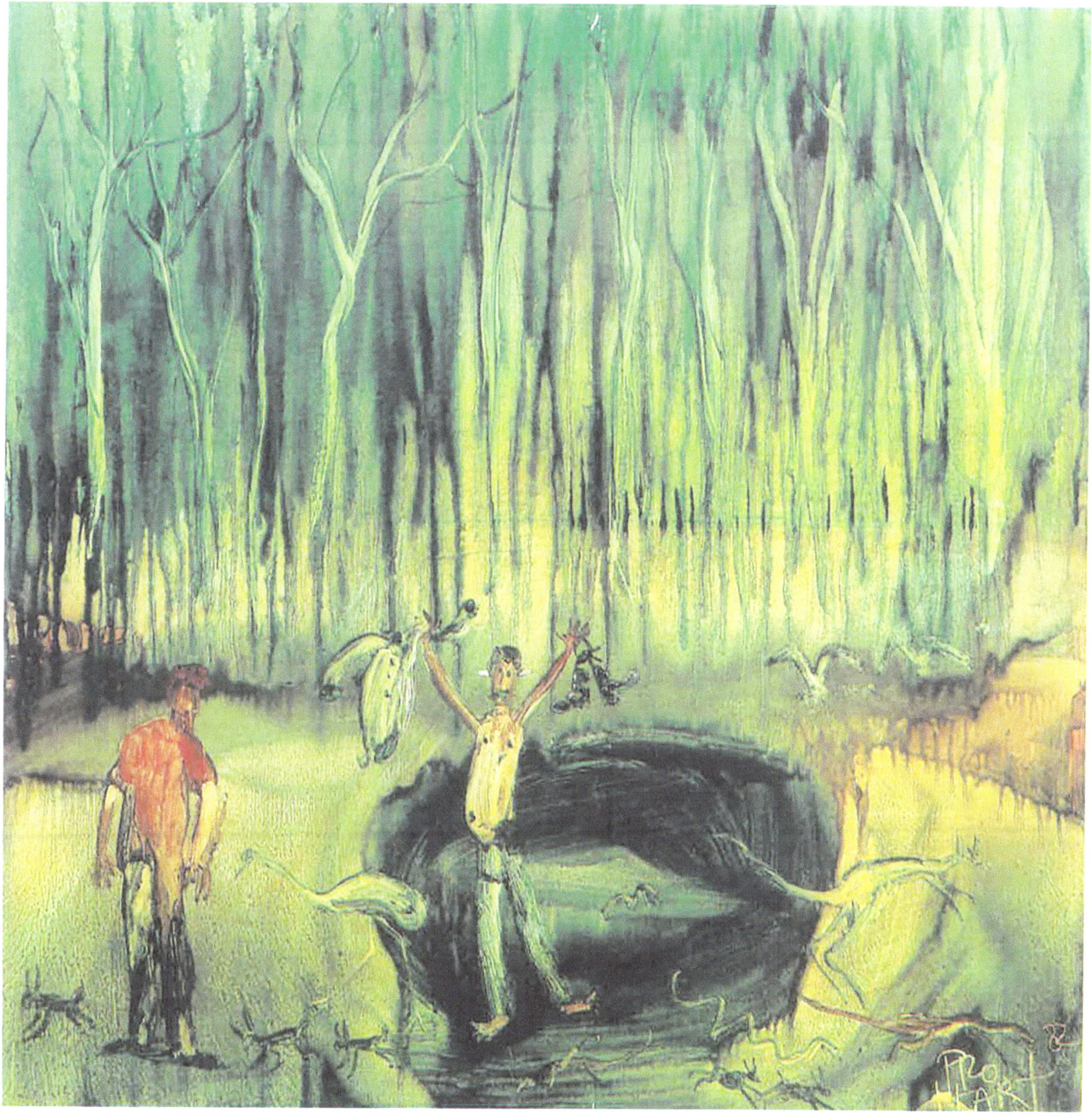

The Counsel of Caiaphas

When the town council met that night,
to contain the crisis called Jesus,
it was meet, right, and proper,
that I, as the priest,
would offer the counsel of God,
for Jesus, this man from the mulga,
was scattering outrageous claims
to be God in the flesh,
conceived in the Dreaming,
a son of the Holy One.

The situation was dangerous
and signs of uprisings were heard
like the hissing of snakes
in the heat,
as poor people trotted on
after this dog from the bush.

There was talk of breaking down buildings
and smashing the house of our God;
there was talk of taking up arms
and leading a bushman's revolt;
there was talk of making him king
and handing his flesh out as bread.

The man was quite mad,
a brute from the bush
like a convict run wild
and filled with a sack full of devils;
when a sheep dog runs wild
there is only one thing to do—
the cur must be killed
before he destroys the whole flock.

It is easy enough
to kill our young men
when they march off with God to war,
but what do we say it is for?

It is easy enough
to stand in a trench
and sacrifice boys to the knife,
but what do we say it is for?

It was easy enough
to see Jesus should die,
like a bushranger riddled with hate,
but what could we say it was for?

So I counselled the council
that one man should die,
die for the peace of his people
and prevent the bloodshed of war . . .

at least,
that is what we said it was for.

John 11:45–53

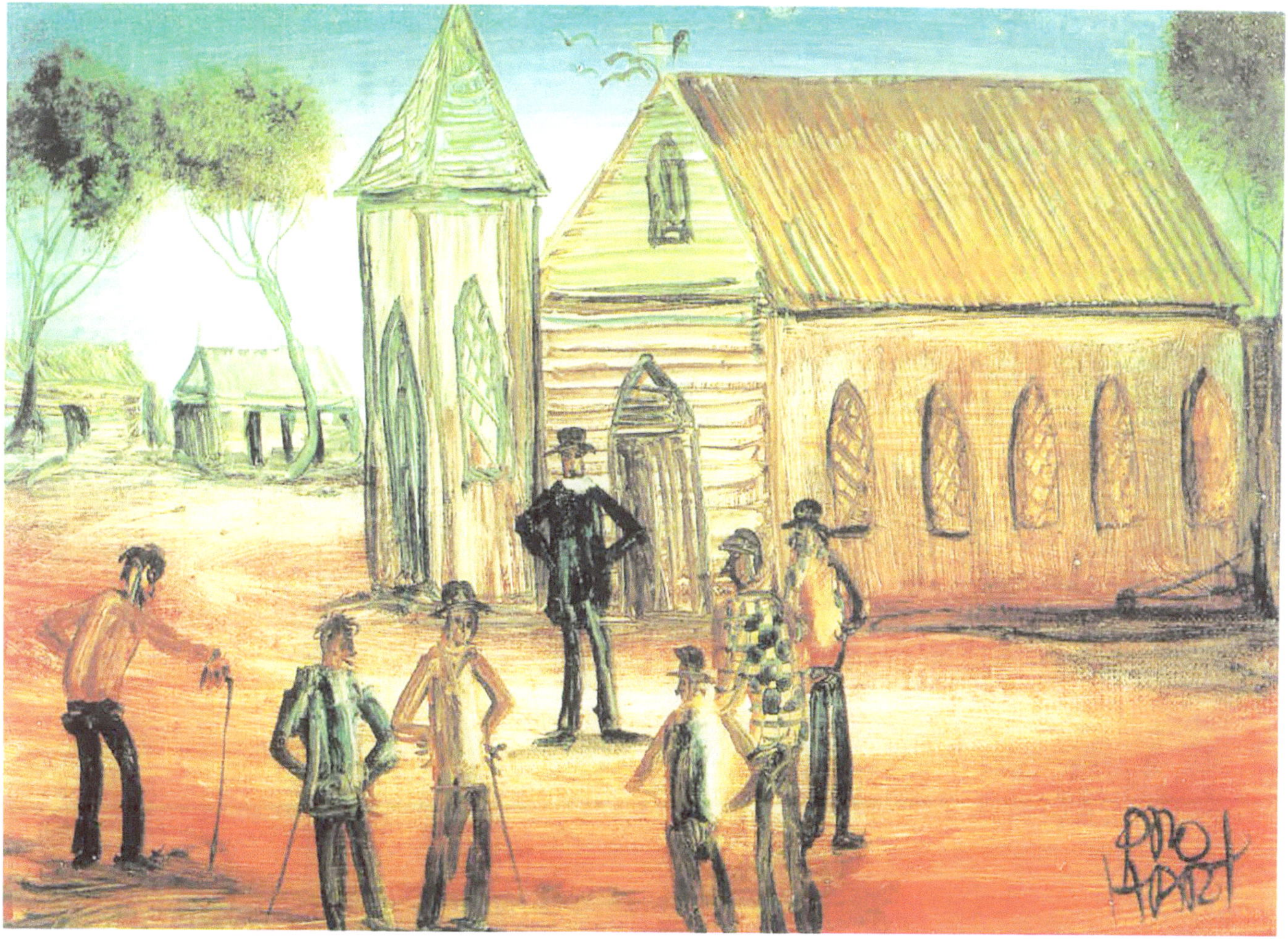

The Love of Mary

The old homestead at Bethany
Was a watering hole
For stockmen and drovers
Left dry by the heat of the track.
At night they would squat
Beneath a tall gum
And tell us their tales
Of taming the fierce world out back.

Round the drovers there hovered
The smell of the dust,
The sweat of the horse,
The taste of greasy grey sheep.
I hung on their stories
In search of a dream,
A man or a mystery,
To lift my soul from its sleep.

> Like a lonely blue crane
> By the edge of the scrub
> I listened each dawn
> For a wind
> That would lift my soul.

You will never know waiting
As a lonely blue crane
Unless you have watched
The fall of a hawk from the sky.
You will never know dreaming
As a woman in pain
Unless you are loved
By men with dust in their eyes.

Of the strangers who stayed here
The Bushman called Jesus
Could speak to my soul
As no lonely traveller before.
He talked of the Dreaming,
A wind sent from God
To make me alive
Like gulls swept high as they soar.

> Like a lonely blue crane
> By the edge of the scrub
> I listened each dawn
> For a wind
> That would lift my soul.

I adored the man Jesus,
My eagle, my king,
My hero gone bush,
A dreamer at one with the sky,
What joy could I give
The man in my soul,
What word of farewell
To one on his journey to die.

I removed from my hope chest
My best scented oil,
And sat where the men
Were washing their dry dusty hands.
I rubbed Jesus' feet
With my oil, with my soul,
My hair flowing down
Like water poured out on the sand.

The rough stockmen felt awkward,
Poor Martha was shocked,
And Lazarus grinned
As Judas preached gifts for the poor.
My Bushman would die,
For he, not the poor,
Would soon leave us all;
My gift was a longing—no more!

> Like a lonely blue crane
> By the edge of the scrub
> I listened each dawn
> For a wind
> That would lift my soul.

John 12:1–8

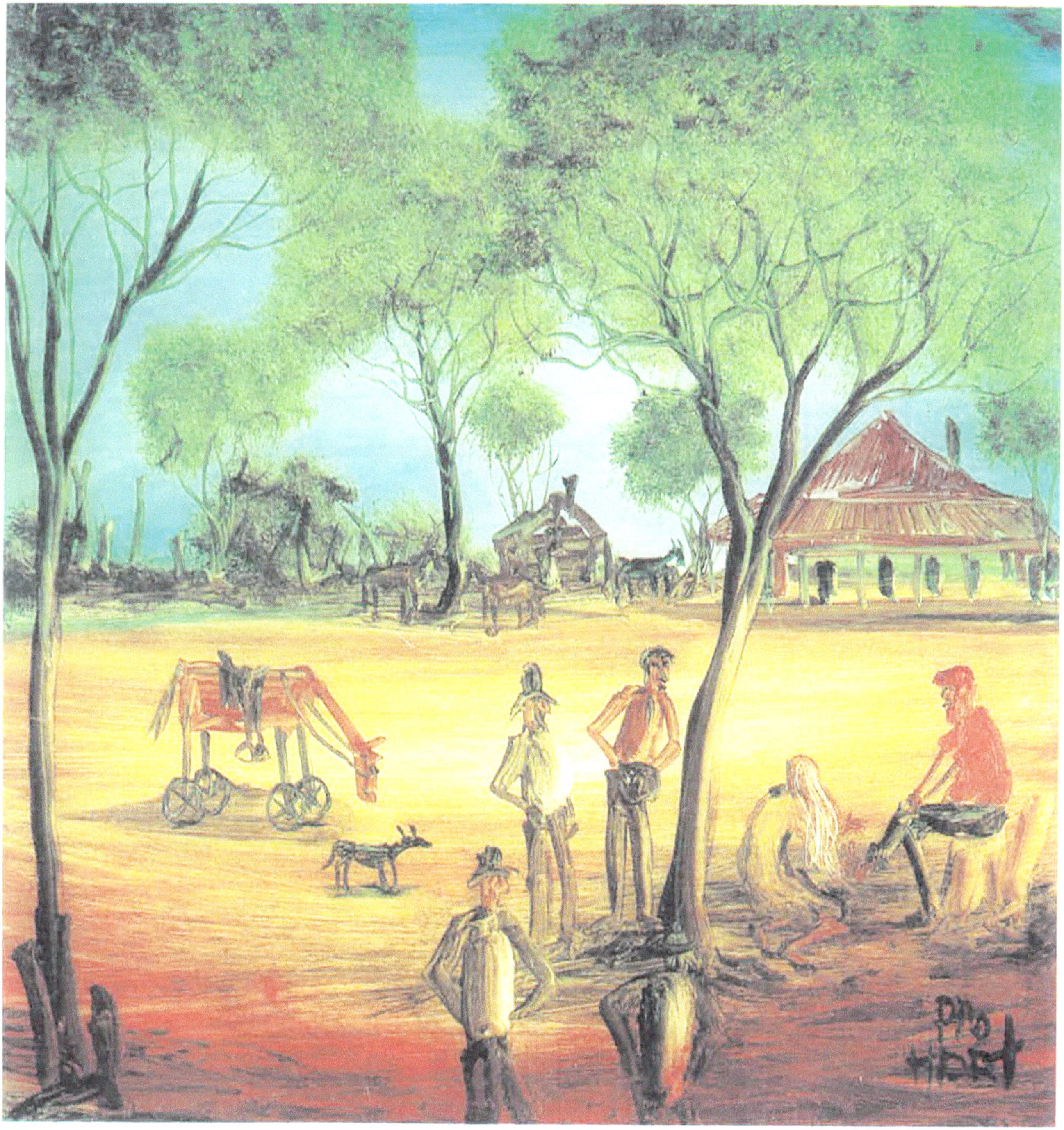

Enter the King of the Bush

Hurry! Hurry!
Come see the parade of freaks,
Men and idiots healed by Jesus
With one swift look of his eyes.
Come see the digger born blind—
He now spies gold like a hawk!
See the crippled old shearer—
He leaps like a new born lamb
And shears like a son of a gun.
See the larrikin Lazarus—
He grins like a cat
That survived nine lives.
Come hear the magic tins
From the wild tin kettling at Cana
Where Jesus turned water to beer.
Come and join in the cheer
Of the jeering jackeroo:

> Hurrah! Hurrah!
> For the mug from the mulga,
> The King of the Bush,
> He'll be lifted up high
> Between the earth and sky
> And his face will tell us the truth.

Hurry! Hurry!
See the wild man from Galilee,
Jesus, the mighty King of the Bush.
Come see his country companions,
His barmaids and bushwackers,
His whalers and bullockies,
And me, the jeering jackeroo,
All coming to town in our glory.
Come see our new bush circus,
Our wild magic mulga show.
You can see devoted old drovers
Unrolling their swags in the dirt
For the Bushman's nag to trample.
You can see beautiful maidens
Like Mary the Magdalene,
Flicking off flies with branches
And elegant emu feathers.
And you can hear the cheer
Of the jeering jackeroo:

> Hurrah! Hurrah!
> For the mug from the mulga,
> The King of the Bush.
> He'll be lifted up high
> Between the earth and the sky
> And his face will tell us the truth.

Hurry! Hurry!
Join the grand celebration
As Jesus enters town.
Watch as Jesus stops the crowd!
Watch as he yells to the sky:
'Is this the way to glory?
Is this the way to die?'
Hear the roar from the heavens,
The thunder of a heavy angel
Calling from God to his son,
'This is the way to glory!
Glory with God on high!'
Hear the miracle man Jesus
Addressing the crowd,
'Come, come see me die;
One day you'll follow me.
Come, see me lifted high
to throw old Satan down.
Come, sing your cheer, your jeer;
Perhaps one day you'll know
The truth in what you sing':

> Hurrah! Hurrah!
> For the mug from the mulga,
> The King of the Bush.
> He'll be lifted up high
> Between the earth and the sky
> And his face will tell us the truth.

Sorry folks,
The miracle man has vanished again,
Lost somewhere in the crowd
With one of his many disguises.
Come back tomorrow!
Perhaps he will perform a sign
Then even you and I can believe . . .
Before the poor chap
Dies!

John 12:9–40

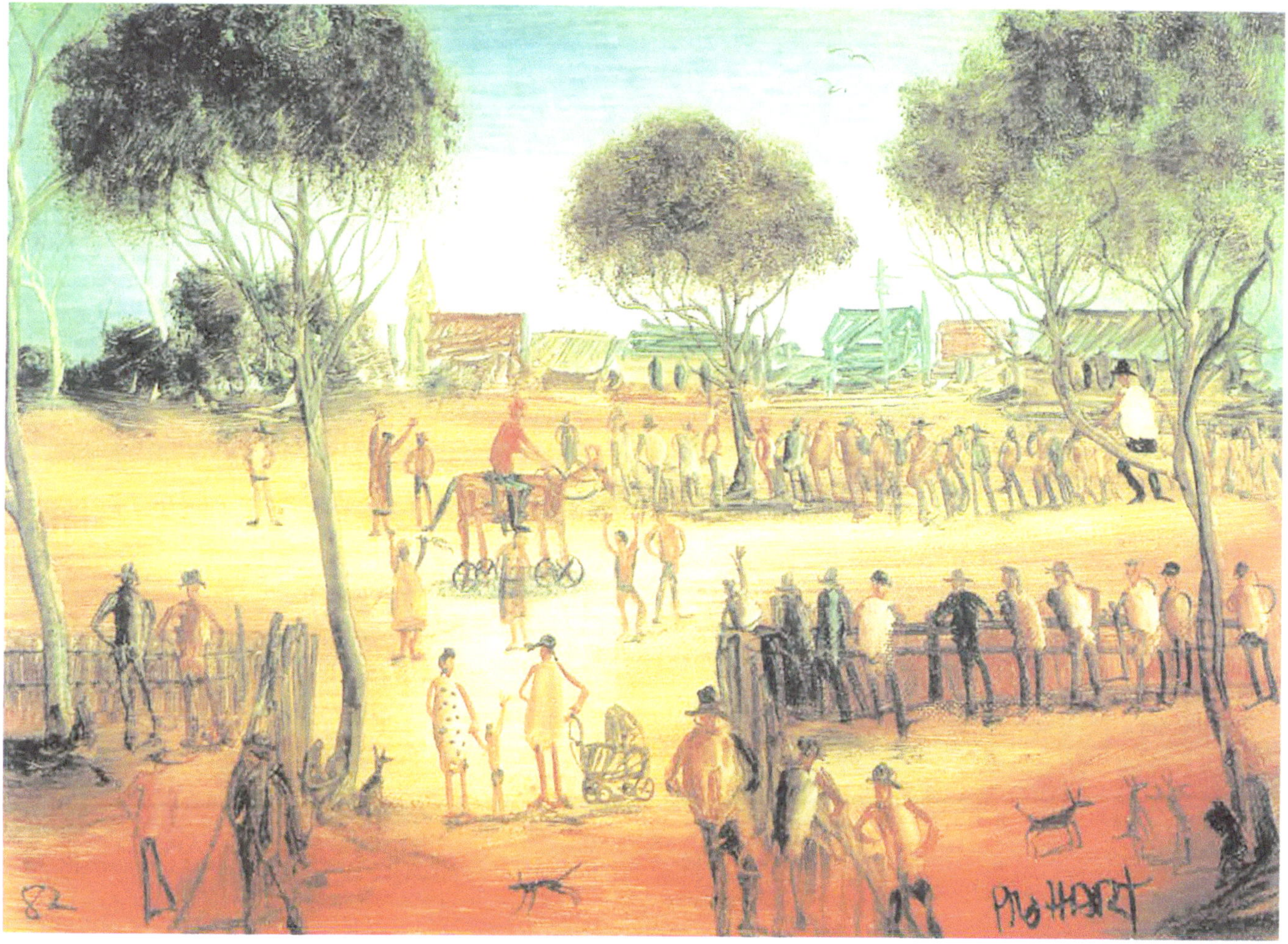

The Anguish of Judas

I loved that man.
I loved his sun-bitten face,
His red prickle beard,
The wild turkey feather stuck in his hat
And the burning pain in his eyes.
I loved his line about sons of light
Overthrowing sons of darkness.
I was ready to fight
All squatters, all troopers,
All evil rulers of night.

He betrayed me, that man!
He betrayed me in front of my mates.
He shouted us rum that night
And made us feel close
Like children long lost out back.
When he handed me the dish
Of our last rabbit stew
He declared to my mates,
That I would dob him in—
A thing I had to do.

He betrayed me. I ran.
He betrayed me, that man.
Just one of those things?
No way!
He did not explain
That fighting sons of darkness
Was more than killing young squatters
Or setting their stables on fire.

He betrayed me. I screamed.
I hated that man.
The devil invaded my soul.
I went to the council
And we went with the troopers
To the camp where Jesus was waiting.

He knew I would come,
Would come with arms,
Was forced to come,
Was led.

With torches aloft
They surrounded my friend,
Kneeling in prayer.

When Jesus stood up
The troopers fell back
As if hit by magpies
Swooping from gum trees above.

They seized my man
Without any fight
And bound him with raw cowhide.

I loved that man.
I loved his sunbitten face.
But he wanted to die.
What else could I do
But turn him in
And suffer the pain in his eyes?

John 18:1–11

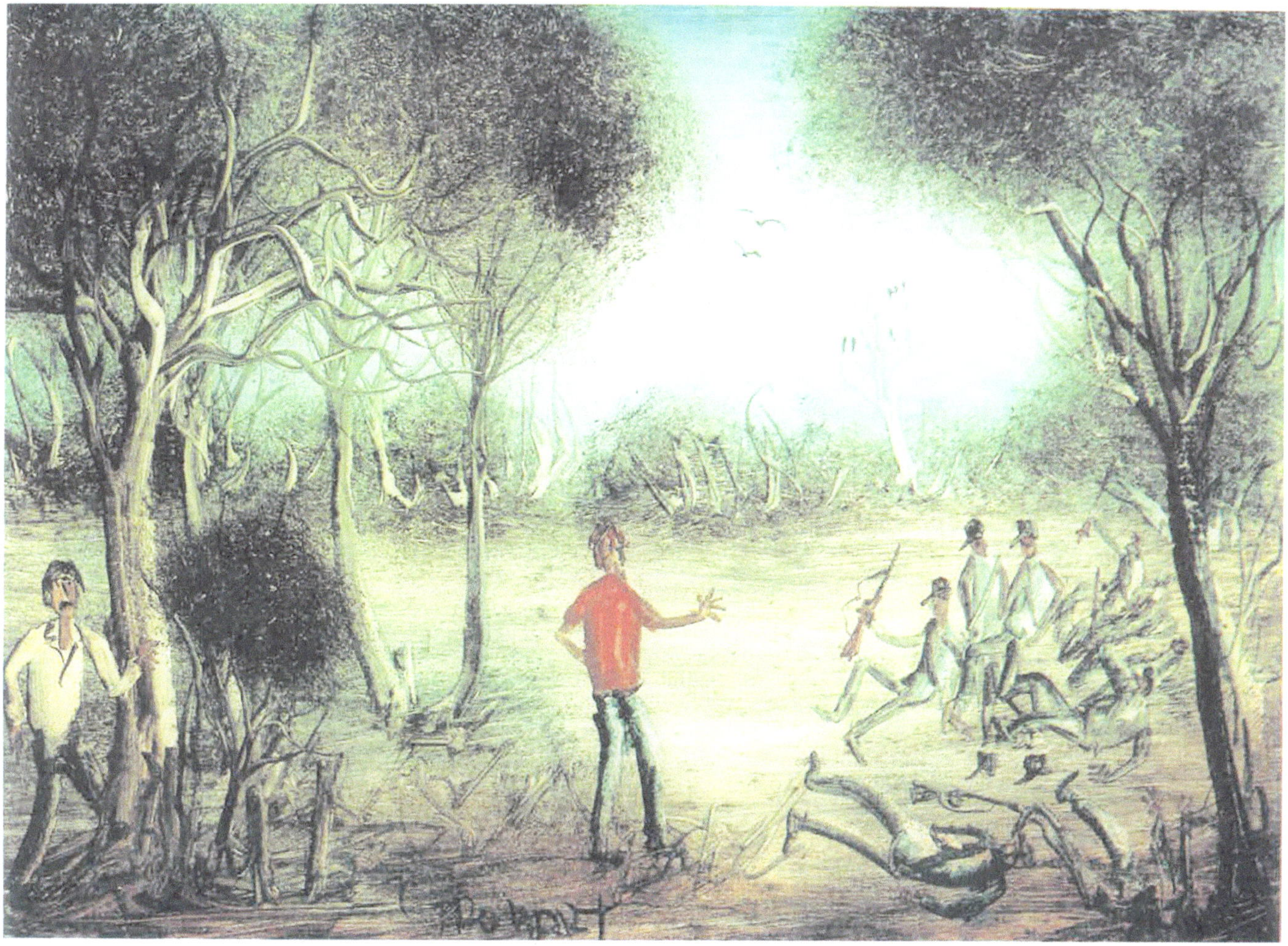

The Pain of Peter

I know how it feels
To fail a friend.

A long forgotten maid,
I work at the house of the priest.
The jokers who come here
For a chat
Are failures like me.

The night they brought in Jesus
For his chat,
We waited outside in the yard
Where the smoke from the fire
Kept biting the edge of our eyes.

Two jokers came near
And stood in the smoke.
One bloke I found later,
Was Peter the whaler,
A mate of the Bushman on trial.

I asked this bloke Peter
What Jesus the Bushman was like.
I hoped he might tell us a yarn
Or one of those tall bush tales
That hovered 'round Jesus like flies.

Peter the whaler said, 'No.
I don't know the man.'
Another cove yelled,
'You've got to be joking.
You rode with his gang.
You're one of his mates.'

'Don't be a fool,' said Peter,
'I wouldn't be seen with the mug.'

Nearby was the priest's altar boy,
Whom Peter had chopped on the ear
When the traps arrested the Bushman
Early that night in the scrub.
The kid blurted, 'Peter.
I saw you. You're Peter.
I saw you back there in the scrub.
You gave me a bloody sore ear.'

'Shut up,' said Peter,
'I don't know the joker at all.'

Laughter burst forth from the trees,
The laughter of cruel kookaburras,
That slashed through his soul
And drove Peter into the scrub,
Heaving with bitter remorse.

I felt what he felt,
The failing,
The pain,
Failing a friend,
Denying his love,
Again and again and again.

I cried
When I saw Peter cry . . .

and our crying was good.

John 18:15–27

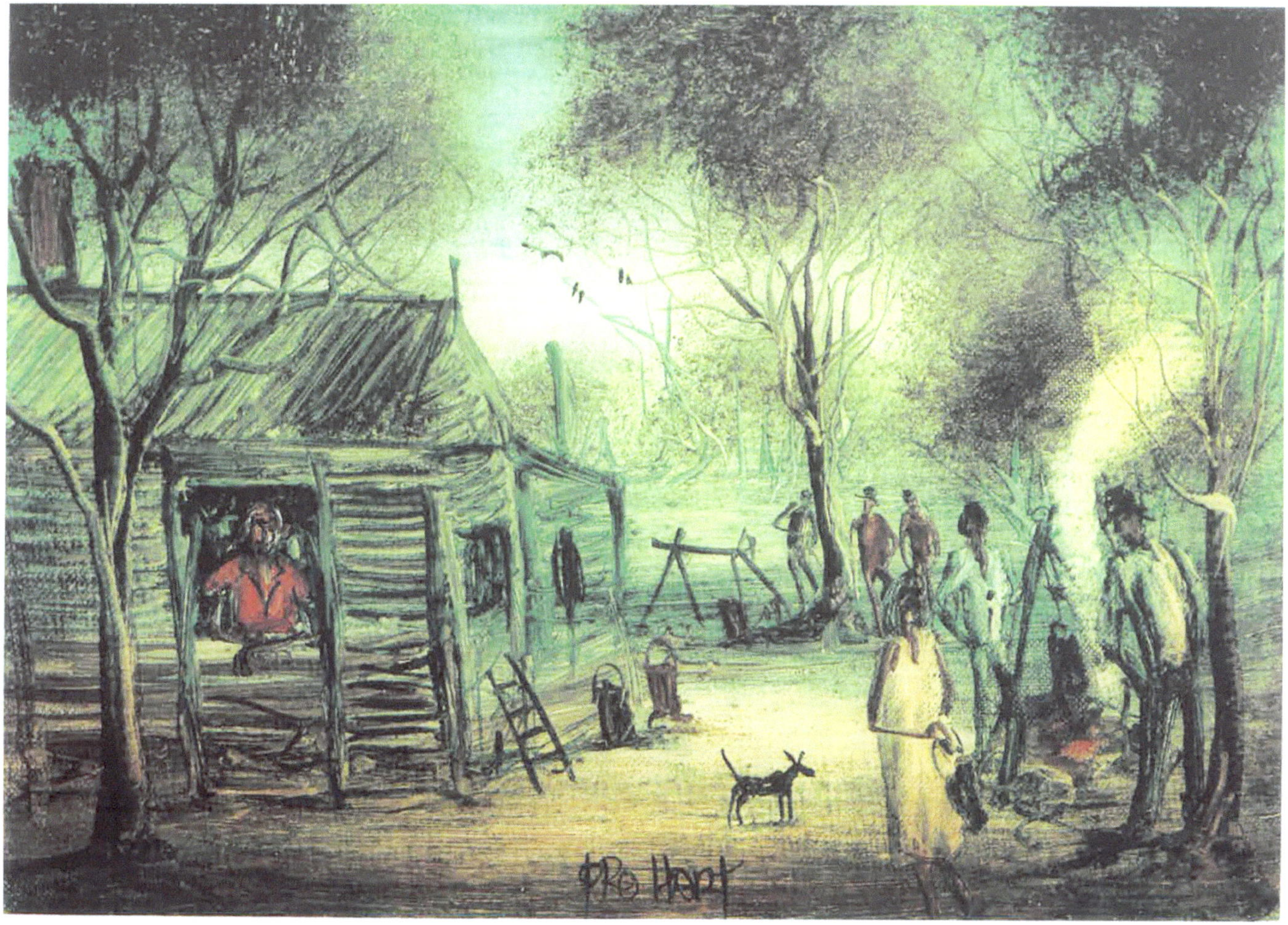
Pro Hart

The Politics of Pilate

In the dry night air,
The cicadas crackling,
Crackling like fire overhead,
The priests called for the death
Of Jesus, the Bushman.

The priests are such prigs.
Why is their God so hard?
Why do they claim like kings
That they alone have the truth?
Why is their faith so barren,
Like breasts sucked dry of their youth.

Why did they want Jesus dead?
Because he upset
Their hold on the truth?
Because be brought God
Close to the weak?

The laws of this land
Do not demand
A man like Jesus should die
For his dreaming.

I decided to play my cards with care
And speak to the Bushman's pride.
'Are you a King?' I asked,
'Lord of some land out back?'

'I am a King,' said Jesus,
'But not like the kings you know,
Who take their people to war.
I come from the Dreaming
To rule the deep bush,
The bush at the heart of our lives.
I'm here to reveal
That truth to you all.'

'Truth! What is truth?'
I retorted.
'Like all the rest
You talk about truth.
It's all a big game
That no one can win—
But we all take the blame.'

I told the town council,
And the crackling pig priests,
I found no crime in their King.
'By our truth,' they intoned,
'the Bushman should die.'

What could I do?
I was for peace, not riots
Or truth.
And Jesus seemed intent
On dying as King of the Bush.

As a gesture of kindness,
Of peace and goodwill,
I set free Barabbas,
A bushranger chap from Outback.
I felt human and warm
As I set that man free,
Trusting that God in his mercy
Would lead him to change his ways
And be human like me.

And Jesus—
Jesus I whipped!
Jesus I condemned to die!

Well, that is what everyone wanted
—even Jesus!

John 18:28–40

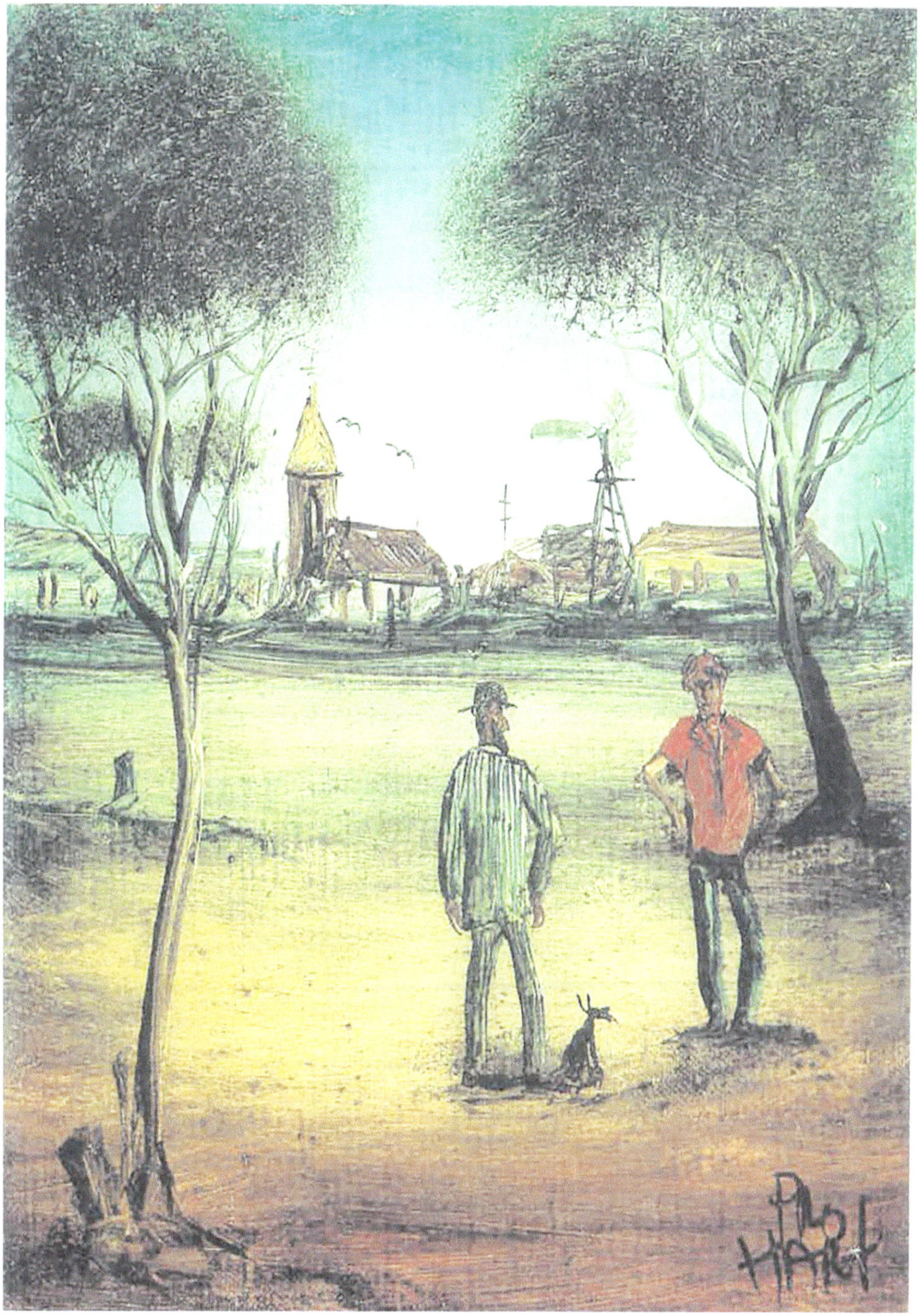

A Chant for Killing

Jesus' face was bleeding
from red whip lashes
when Pilate presented him
to the crowd for their homage
and their chant of:

Hail the King!
Hail the Bush!
Hail the King of the Bush!

The crown on Jesus' head
was spinifex and wire grass,
the robe on his shoulders
a ragged rug of wallaby hide,
the gold brocade
a spray of withered wattle,
his symbols of office,
a whip
and a long digger's shovel,
the chant in his honour:

Hail the King!
Hail the Bush!
Hail the King of the Bush!

The wise priests,
their fangs spitting hatred
into the soul of the man
who exposed their greed,
wanted the Bushman dead
for claiming to be God's son . . .
and knowing more than they,
as subtly they changed the chant
to cries of:

Kill the King!
Free the Bush!
Kill the King of the Bush!

The lusty crowd
barked for human blood,
a demon force within
led them to turn
on one they once loved
for not rebelling with arms
and filling their pockets with gold
as the chant became a cheer:

Kill the King!
Free the Bush!
Kill the King of the Bush!

Pilate, the dingo,
pacing back and forth,
sought a way of escape
to free the Bushman,
a man he knew in his heart
did not deserve to die.
'I find him innocent,'
cried Pilate in pain.
'Kill him!' they yelled.
'He is your king,'
Pilate replied.
'Kill this traitor,' they cried,
'Our king is over the seas!'
As the chant for killing swelled:

Kill the King!
Free the Bush!
Kill the King of the Bush!

And we, his mates, his sheep,
watched the world go wild
and evil race like fire;
frozen by our fear,
we heard the chant for death
rise louder and higher:

Kill the King!
Free the Bush!
Kill the King of the Bush!

Jesus stood silent
in that parody of royalty,
as an ugly evil longed
to consume him with its lust
until it lapped his blood
in cold anticipation
waiting for the kill,
calling for the kill,
lusting for the kill,
with its chant of:

Kill the King!
Free the Bush!
Kill the King of the Bush!

John 19:1–16

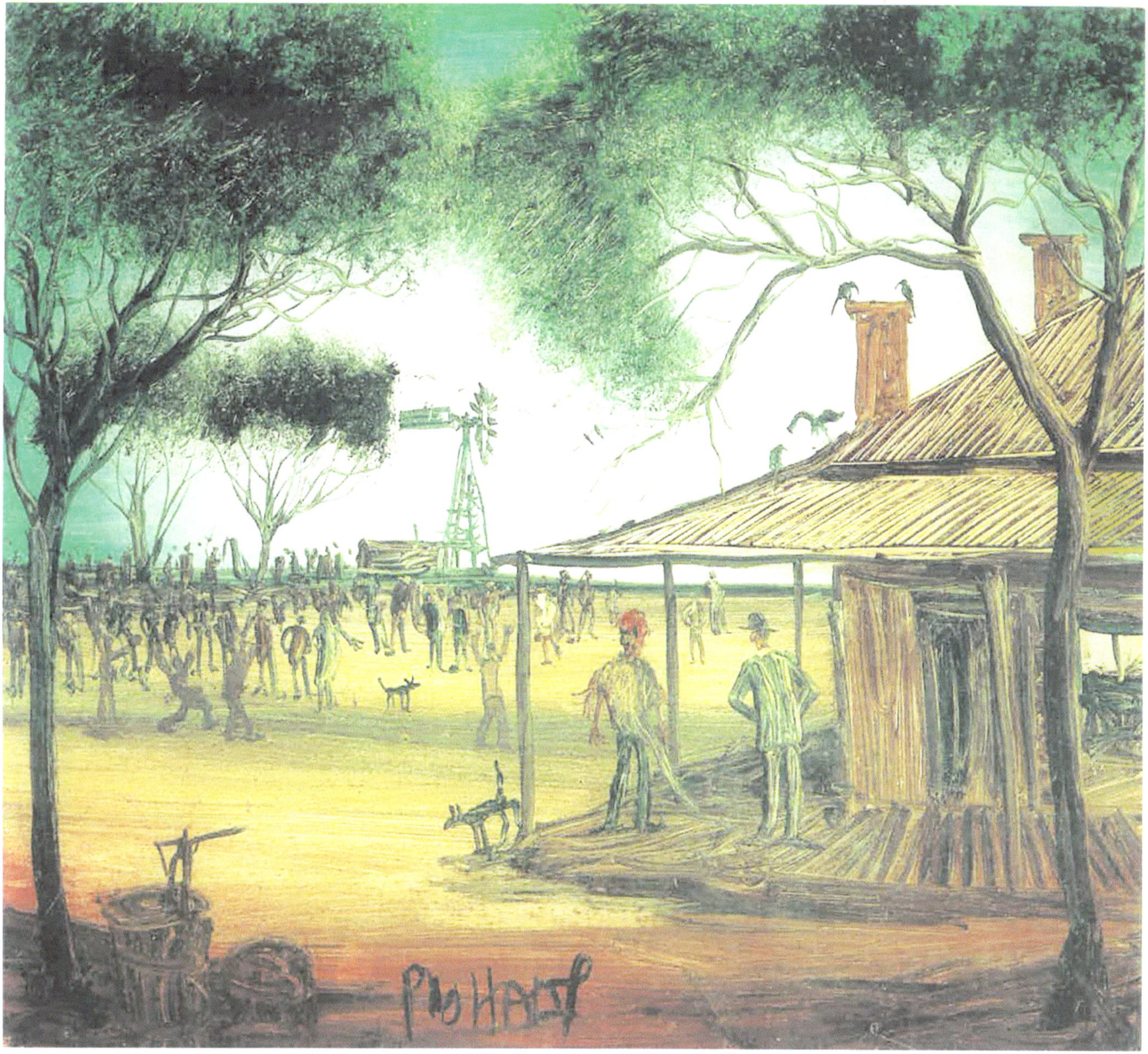

She's Hot on the Hill

At the sentence of death
the verdict was passed
through the heat:

She's a hot one today.
She's a scorcher, alright.
She's hot on the crown of the hill.

He was led to a mound
where death is alive
on the hill.
From a bleached desert tree
he was lifted up high
in the heat.

The name carved in bark
read 'King of the Bush'
on the hill.
From the sun to the sand
the word was passed on
through the heat:

She's a hot one today.
She's a scorcher, alright.
She's hot on the crown of the hill.

By his side in the sun
two bushrangers hung
on the hill.
Stripped naked of clothes
his life was exposed
to the heat.

From the slow setting sun
rose the wings of a throne
on the hill.
And the verdict was passed
as the Bushman was killed
By the heat:

She's a hot one today.
She's a scorcher, alright.
She's hot on the crown of the hill.

John 19:17–22

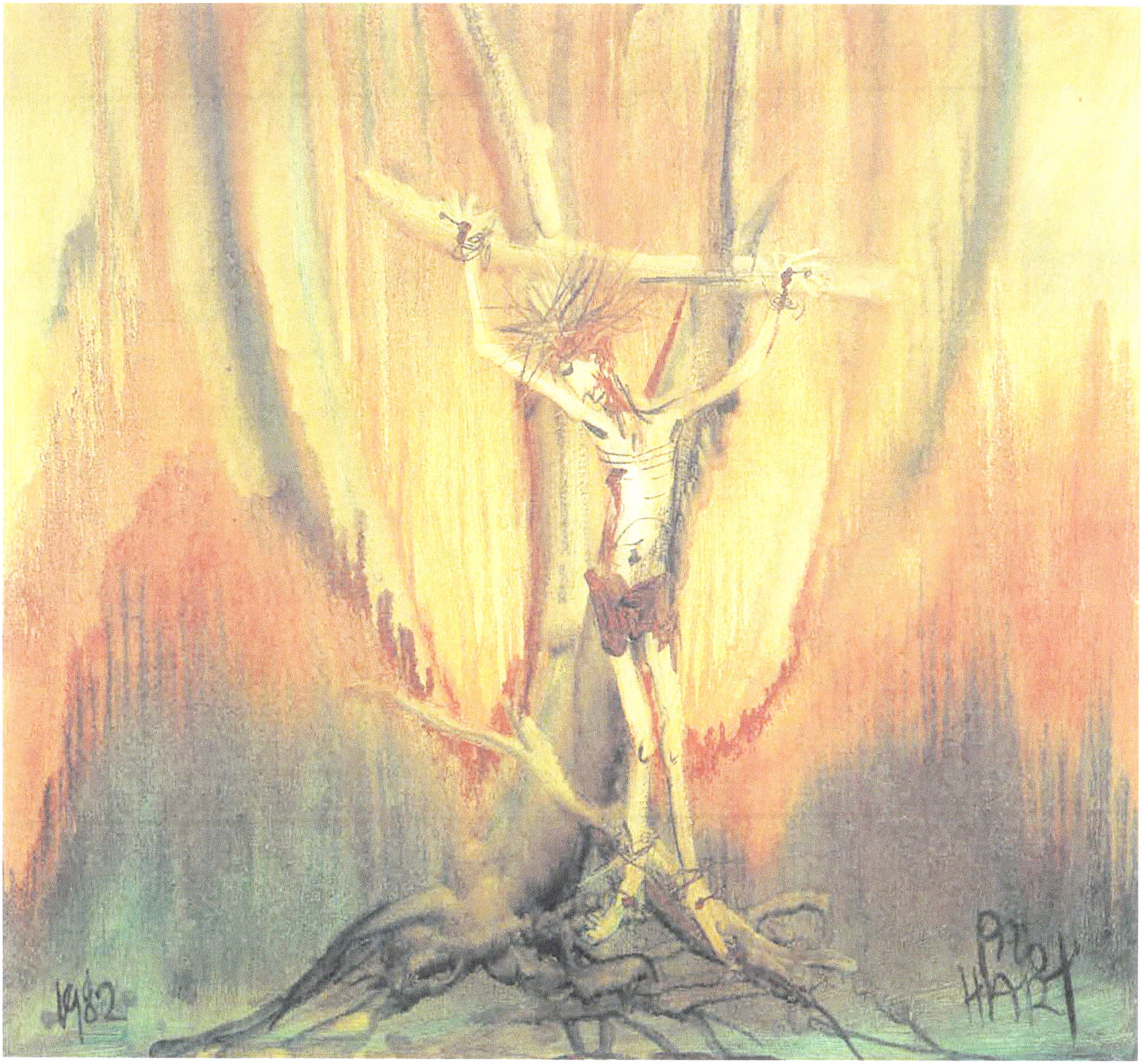
1982

I am a Mother

I am a mother, a tree
standing tall in the sun,
climbed by rough men
and windswept by memories.

I recall
the distant father of my child,
the chill shadow running through me,
the birth splitting my trunk,
and the tales of chattering angels.

I recall
the loss of a son gone bush,
a child beyond arm's reach,
a boy grown bushman,
grown wild with miracles . . .
and the evil,
always the evil hovering close,
close to my child.

Was I chosen to be mother
of a cruel exchange,
mother of a man who sought death
in place of my wisdom?

He took on the world
with his eyes,
burning off masks,
and calling hollow souls
to find love born in pain,
to find love in his death,
the love of God
rising like the wind,
against rolling clouds
of guilt and shame.

High on the hill,
poised to die in the sun
he called to me
and one of his mates,
named John.

'Mother,' he cried,
'Take John for your son.
And John, my good friend,
Take Mary, my mother, as yours.'

One son, one pain,
in exchange for another.

In the end
he chose to die.
He took a drink,
bowed his head to the sky
offered his spirit to God
and shouted,
'It is done.'

Through the bush it echoed,
like thunder before rain,
pounding, pounding the heavens,
'It is done.
It is done.
It is done.'

Deep in my aching body
I heard my womb reply,
'I am mother.
I am mother.
I have only now begun.'

John 19:23–30

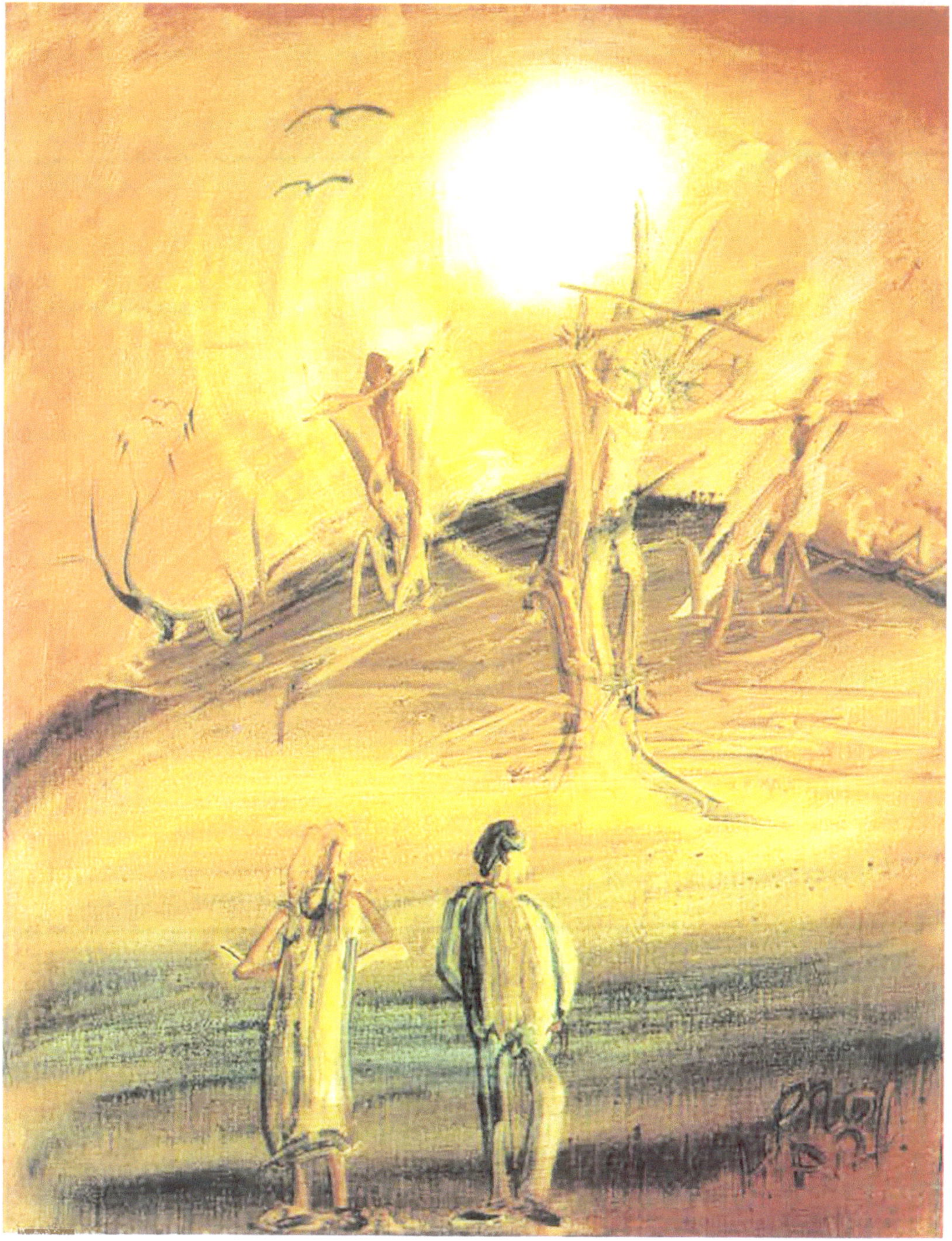

The Lament of Nicodemus

We took down his body,
His whip beaten body,
We looked at the face of his dying,
And we moaned

And we moaned,
Like a curlew out calling the moon
And we moaned
And we moaned till the dawn.

We took off his bush crown,
His sharp sweaty bush crown,
The mark of disgrace he was wearing,
And we moaned

And we moaned
Like a curlew out calling the moon
And we moaned
And we moaned till the dawn.

Far back in a cave hole,
A bat haunted cave hole,
We laid up his body for sleeping
And we moaned

And we moaned
Like a curlew out calling the moon
And we moaned
And we moaned till the dawn.

Engraved in the cave hole,
The black haunted cave hole,
Were images left from the Dreaming
And they moaned

And they moaned
Like a curlew out calling the moon
And they moaned
And they moaned till the dawn.

We bound up his body,
His sun savoured body,
And left it for waking one morning,
And we moaned

And we moaned
Like a curlew out calling the moon
And we moaned
And we moaned till the dawn.

Outside 'neath the gum trees,
The wide weeping gum trees,
We cracked his old stockwhip in parting,
And it moaned

And it moaned
Like a curlew out calling the moon
And it moaned
And it moaned till the dawn.

John 19:38–42

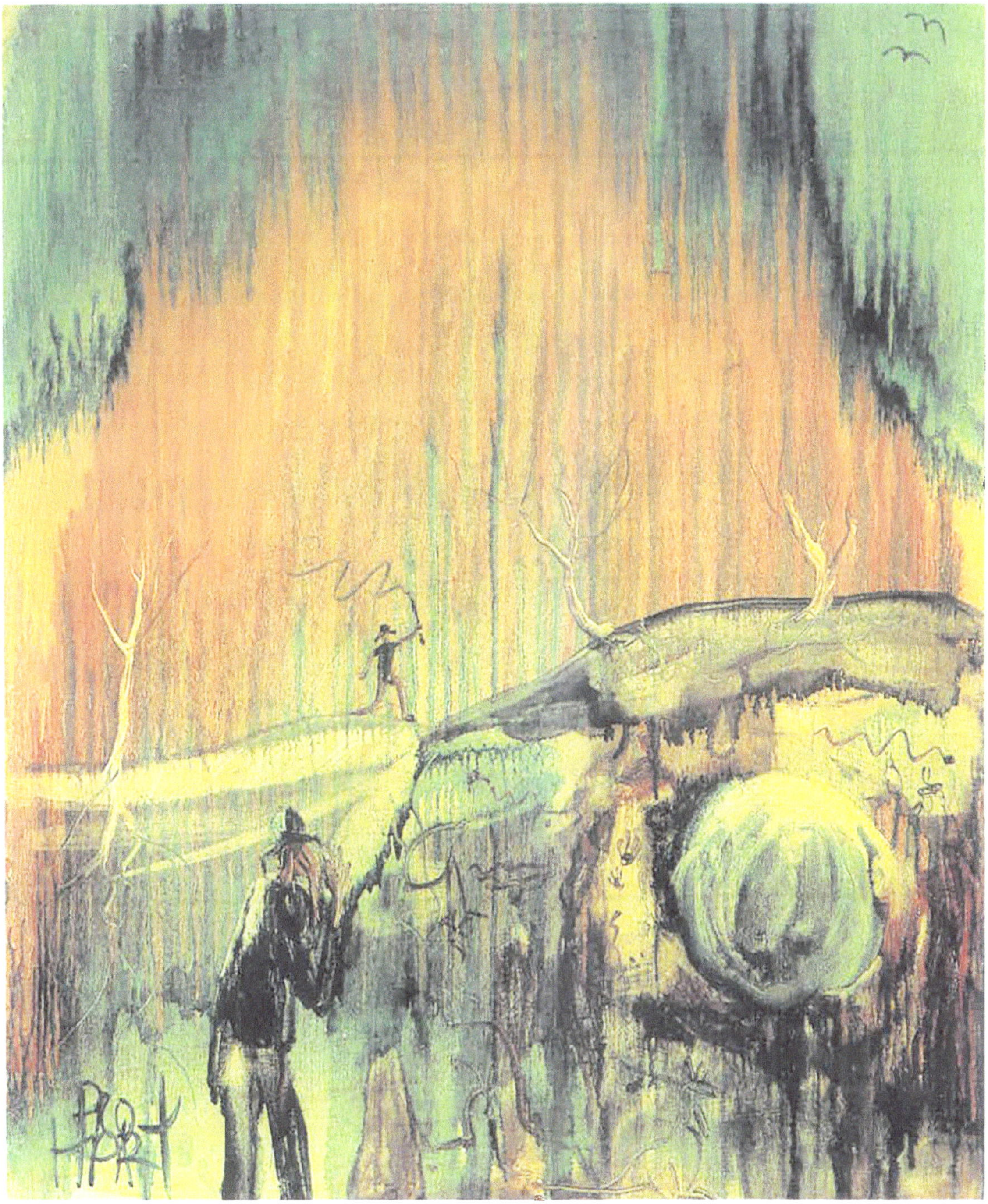

I Could Not Believe My Eyes

I could not believe my eyes
when I saw him
lifted high
on a burning hill to die
like one enthroned in the sun.

I wept,
an empty woman
by an open tomb.
A deserted queen
by an empty cave,
I called to the void.

Two angels stood
like native companions,
brolgas, ibis white,
asking why I was weeping.

Clumsy guardians
of the desert dead!
They could see
the body of Jesus was gone,
stolen like carrion
by human dogs.

A curious digger
asked the same fool question,
'Why are you weeping, woman?'

'Where's he gone?'
I cried,
'Back of the cave?
Under a mound?
Deep in the shaft of a mine?'

'Mary,' said the digger,
and I could not believe my ears.

That voice,
like wind rising,
like driven rain
tumbling down again
from the hill where he died—
that voice
of my King!

I could not believe my eyes
when I saw the digger,
his red prickle beard,
and his eyes.

Those eyes,
like the flame of the sun,
like the campfire low
dancing the shadows of night—
the eyes
of the bloke called Jesus!

'Don't hold me,' said Jesus,
'as you did out back.
I'm leaving your bush
to be with my Father
deep in the land of the Dreaming.
There when I meet you once more
you will hold me as never before.'

I raced off in joy.
I ran like a girl.
I told all I found
the bushman called Jesus
was back.

And would you believe,
the mulga rejoiced,
the red parrots sang,
and the desert pea
bloomed with delight . . .
only my friends were surprised
and would not believe
my eyes.

John 20:11–18

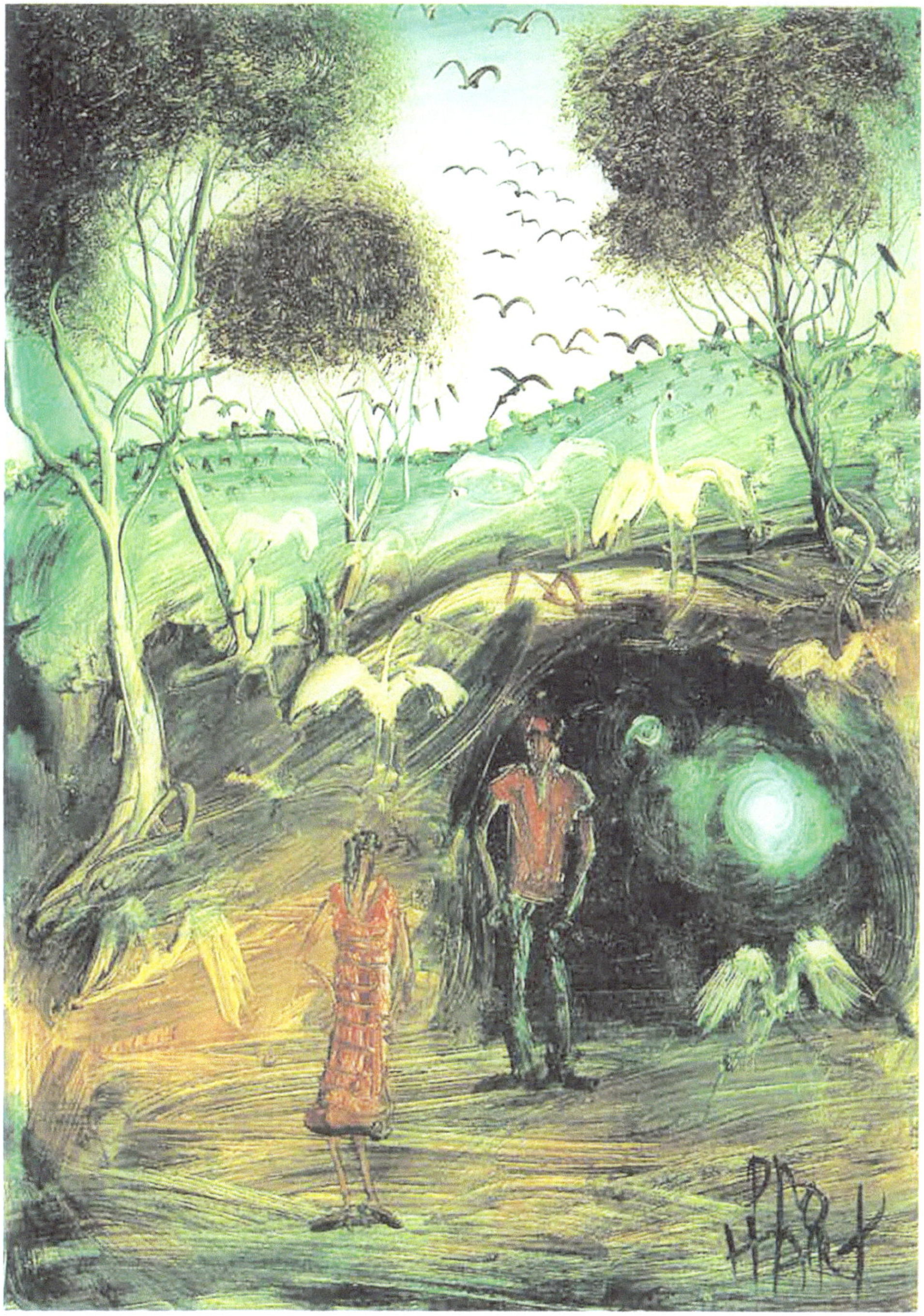

Come Share a Damper with Me

After the hot day on the hill,
the denying. the dying,
the moan of the ghost gums,
the killing of country dreams,
and the burial of the Bushman,
we were lost.

Under the gaping night sky
we returned to the river we knew,
the friendly fishing holes,
and the sad gentle frogs.
The river knew our pain
as it flowed on down
to be lost in the salty sea.
The river gums knew,
the elegant ibis
and the chattering parrots knew,
knew our emptiness.

At dawn a man called from the bank.
"I hear they're biting upstream."

We rowed upstream
where the big ones struck,
hitting our lines like lightning,
just as they had before
when Jesus had given his cue
and the boat was loaded with cod.

As we rowed back to camp
a light filtered down through the trees
as if heaven were sharing a secret
and hovering close to the ground.

The man on the bank was singing
beside a small campfire.
His voice on the water
sent a ripple of chills
through the soft morning air.

I leapt up. I cried.
I exploded inside.
It was Jesus.
He was standing right there
and blazing with life.
It was true.
He was living.

The screeching galahs
like angels in chorus
called every creature
to cheer for our mate,
for the bloke we call Jesus
and join in the song he sang:

Come share a damper with me.
Down under a coolibah tree.
Long by the billabong.
I am the morning song.
Come share a damper with me.

Come drink this new wine with me,
Red blood that flows from a tree.
I am the risen one,
Red as the morning sun.
Come drink my red wine with me.

Come drove the back roads with me,
Explore what mateship can be.
Love me and live with me,
Give and forgive with me.
Come drove God's back roads with me.

Come die in the desert with me,
We'll taste an old mystery.
You are the falling grain,
I am the living rain.
Come rise from the desert with me.

Come make the sun rise with me,
Out back where the silence is free,
I am the dawn above;
I am the depth of love.
Come make the sun rise with me.

Come share a damper with me,
Down under a coolibah tree.
'Long by the billabong,
1 am the morning song.
Come share a damper with me.

John 21:1–23

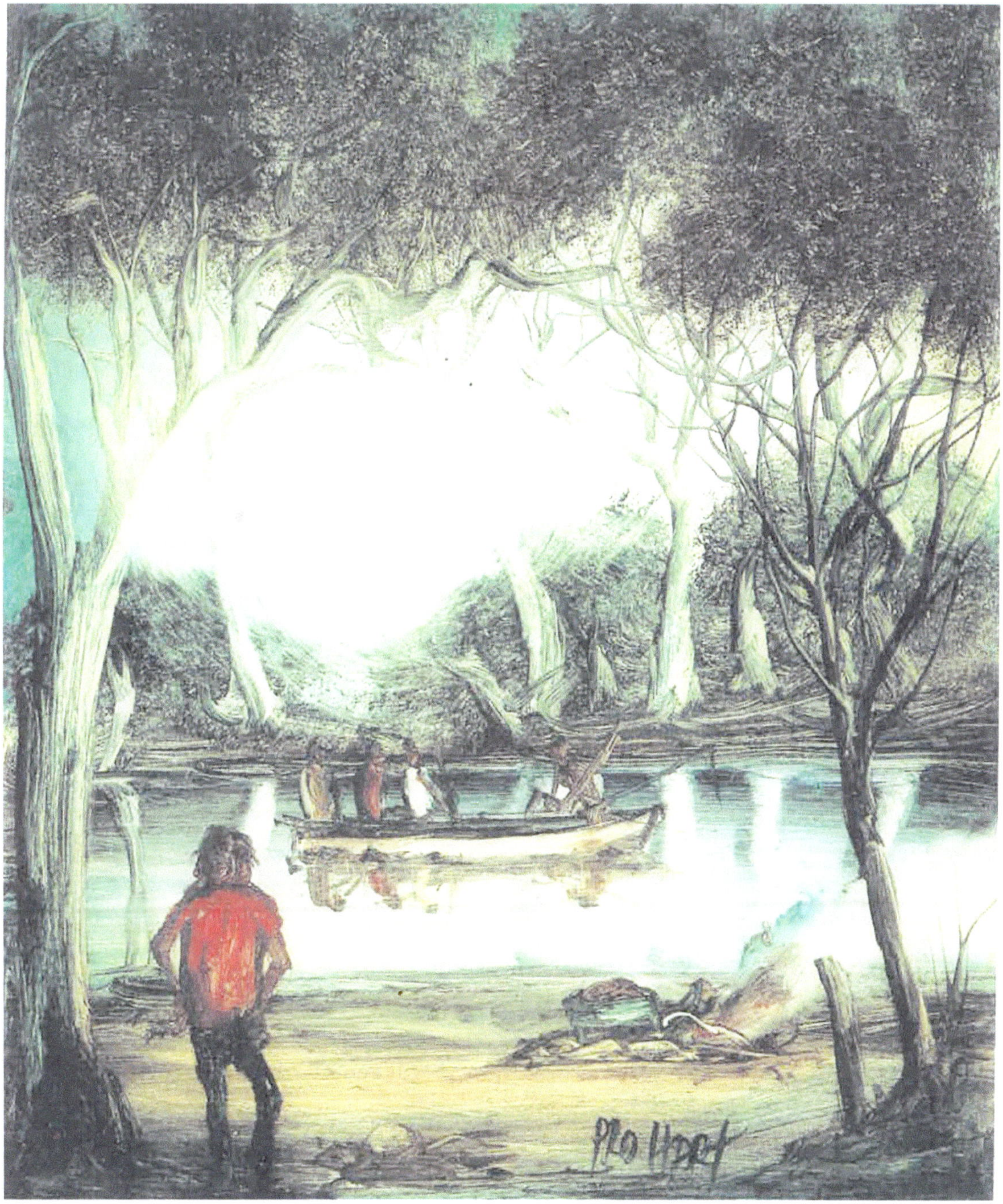
PRO HART

CPSIA information can be obtained
at www.ICGtesting.com
Printed in the USA
LVHW071325300322
714644LV00002B/23